Testimony
of a
'Whatnot'

Published by

Ulster Friends Home Mission
2008

First Edition 2008

Published by
Ulster Friends Home Mission

༄ ༄

The Home Mission
is a part of the
Ulster Quarterly Meeting of the Religious Society of Friends
in Ireland (widely known as Quakers)

Printed by

Sam Robinson Printing & Business Systems
8a Bachelors Walk, Lisburn BT28 1XJ

Contents

Front cover – Pre-partition India
Insert – the author as a girl.

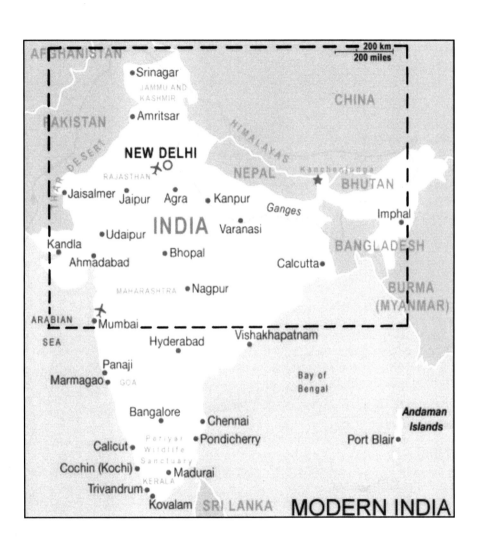

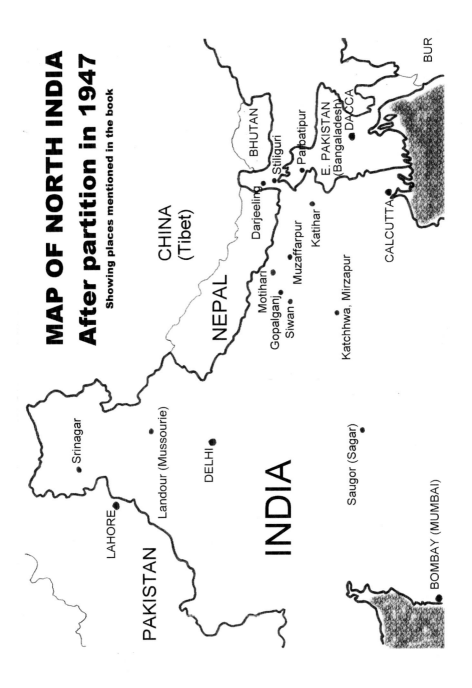

MAP OF NORTH INDIA
After partition in 1947
Showing places mentioned in the book

PAKISTAN

Srinagar

LAHORE

Landour (Mussourie)

DELHI

INDIA

CHINA
(Tibet)

NEPAL

Darjeeling

BHUTAN

Stiliguri

Parbatipur

Motihari

Gopalganj

Siwan

Muzaffarpur

Katihar

E. PAKISTAN
(Bangaladesh)

DACCA

Katchhwa, Mirzapur

CALCUTTA

Saugor (Sagar)

BOMBAY (MUMBAI)

BUR

PREFACE

The life of Elizabeth Pritchard, known to her friends as Betty, spanned almost a century which encompassed great strides in technology, two world wars, and major social change. Her perspective was from a working life spent almost entirely in India as a missionary; first from 1930 as a young single lady working with the Bible Churchman's Missionary Society (BCMS), and then after her marriage to Herbert Pritchard in 1939 with the Regions Beyond Missionary Union (RBMU). Unlike many of her colleagues Betty had no professional qualification or skill, this giving rise to the humorous title 'Whatnot' which is used in a typically self deprecating manner. She also often refers to short comings in her personality, but God revealed in her a special gift of writing; and the material she produced was not only used in India, but also in many other countries. So it was a joy to discover a few years ago that Betty had written an autobiography. Some of our committee then spent many months transcribing the text from thin faintly typed and often roughly annotated sheets on to computer. The resulting file had gaps, errors, and inconsistencies that required painstaking proofing. Helen Kinkead undertook a major part of this task, even though she was enduring the unpleasant side-effects of cancer treatment. Apart from corrections, some alterations were made, but we trust they are faithful to Betty's objective and style. On completion, we were grateful that Leslie Kerr devoted much time and expertise preparing the book for printing.

The finished work is an excellent read. It may appear old fashioned to some, yet it is faithful and honest to its time. Herbert and Betty were missionaries, a term which is not only out of fashion, but is now sometimes used disparagingly. Today organisations are keen on 'Mission Statements'; yet the statement of Jesus "Go throughout the whole world and preach the gospel to all people," (Mark 16:15) was initially greeted by Betty with some trepidation. However looking back on her life and the consequences of the decision to follow God's call, Betty leaves us in no doubt about 'all the wonderful things the Lord has done for me'. The reader of this book will find inspiration in the way in which God deals with us patiently on a personal level, only requiring us to have faith and belief in Jesus, finding unique tasks for us to perform, always answering prayer in His own way and time, and graciously providing the deep love and peace which comes from the indwelling of His Holy Spirit.

After her marriage Betty joined the Religious Society of Friends; her vocal ministry whilst on furlough and then in the period of retirement with Herbert in Lisburn, plus her prayers when restricted in later life, brought much blessing to Friends. She also influenced many young people, especially through her 'practical talks' at Moyallon Camps, and in later life had a pivotal role in a women's prayer and bible study group in Lisburn.

Naturally an autobiography is personal, but Betty's story is far from that modern preoccupation with 'self'. It is about a rarer commodity — self sacrifice and service.

Martin K Mail
Chairman – Ulster Quarterly Meeting Home Mission Committee,
The Religious Society of Friends in Ireland.

We would like to dedicate the publishing of this book to
Helen Mary Kinkead, 17th November 1943 – 22nd April 2007.

TESTIMONY OF A WHATNOT

Author's Note

Describing the European staff of a mission hospital a young doctor once said: "We have two doctors, three sisters, one pharmacist and two whatnots."

I was one of the whatnots, an evangelist, and a non-medical in a medical world. It was an interesting life and I often felt tempted to write some sort of autobiography but it was not until I was lying in a London hospital after a major operation that I felt a real urge to begin. My Daily Light told me that the date was the 11th November 1970, exactly 40 years to the day since I first set foot in India. A verse of scripture came vividly to mind: "You shall remember all the way the Lord your God has led you these forty years in the wilderness, to humble you..." (Deut.8:2) I took the Word to myself and began to recollect all the way the Lord had led me.

In the spring of the following year, immobilised by a broken ankle and unable to return to India on the date planned, I had ample leisure in which to think and to remember. It was then while reading the Living Bible version of what I call the Psalm for Senior Citizens, Psalm 71, that these words struck me forcibly:

I thought to myself: 'Well, I can tell the present generation of all the wonderful things the Lord has done for me but the only way I have of telling their children yet unborn is to write them down.'

I thought at first of adopting my usual medium, the Christian novel, but if I had done so, many would have said: 'Of course, Joan (or Meg or Sue) is herself; she is writing her own life story.' So I felt I might as well be honest and acknowledge that it is my own soul I am laying bare. This is therefore not a novel. I have told the truth as I saw it; and nothing but the truth, but not the whole truth. There are experiences in everybody's life which cannot be discussed without involving other people. I feel that, while I have every right to lay bare my own weaknesses and failures, I have no right to expose other people's.

Contrary to what most people will believe, attempting to write any sort of autobiography can be a very humbling experience. I realize that the constant use of the first person singular seems to give the lie to this; nevertheless it is true. For instance, one must dig out all the old diaries and commonplace books that were kept since youth and, reading them, become suddenly embarrassed. Was I ever really as silly as this, or as intolerant and loathsomely pious? Such heart searching makes me humbly grateful to the friends and colleagues of those early years for their kindness and forbearance, and so marvel that they are still my friends.

Though many of my missionary colleagues will never read this record, I dedicate it to them with love and gratitude, especially to my husband, without whose help it could not have been written.

Elizabeth Pritchard

TESTIMONY OF A WHATNOT

CHAPTER ONE

Prologue

The S.S. *City of Paris* had come triumphantly through the Bay of Biscay with hardly a roll and having turned the corner of Spain was headed for the Mediterranean.

On this bright October morning in 1930 her port decks were deserted. Passengers who were not still in their cabins or in the dining room were leaning on the starboard rail gazing at a long brown shoreline to the south. Africa had crept into view while we were at breakfast. Leaning on the rail beside me was a girl called Ada who I knew was on her way to some Mission station in Africa.

'There is the land of your adoption!' I said lightly. I glanced at her and what I saw made me turn away again embarrassed. She was gazing at the shoreline with the look of one who sees a beatific vision.

'Africa, at last' she breathed, her hands clasped in ecstasy.

After a moment or two I left her, afraid that she might see the exasperation that must be evident on my face. I felt she was being theatrical and my North Country soul revolted against anything I considered affected. But I didn't know why I should also be feeling deflated and somehow guilty. I slipped in beside one of our Mission party and told her what I had seen. 'I shan't look like that when we sight the shores of India.' I said gloomily. And I knew at that moment why I felt guilty.

Edith looked down at me (she was a good nine inches taller) and smiled indulgently. 'You're enjoying this voyage, aren't you?'

'I wish it would never end!' I said. And then I wondered why I had spoken so vehemently.

Was I enjoying the voyage so much? It had begun badly for me. The car taking me to Liverpool had broken down on the road and I had arrived at the docks on an egg lorry, half an hour before we were due to sail. The Mission representative, almost tearing his hair out, was not amused by the sight of our minister friend climbing down from among the egg crates. While this episode had shortened the distressing moments of farewell it had added poignancy and sorrow. So many people had come to see me away, some by train, and they must have been anxious.

We sailed out of Liverpool into a stormy sunset. After all these years I can still see that crowd of relatives and friends, their faces livid in the strange eerie light, among them my patient little Mother trying not to cry, my Father and my brother standing head and shoulders above the rest. Nothing in my experience since has equalled the agony of watching the gap widen between dockside and ship, between myself and Mother and Father, knowing that five years must elapse before we would come together again.

More disaster followed our departure. We were hardly across the harbour bar when we ran into bad weather. Three of the four of us in our cabin lay for two days in acute misery while the ship lurched down the coast of England and across the Channel. We rolled from side to side in our bunks or, for a change, felt our heads sink and our feet rise in the air, hovering thus until the ship, shuddering, righted itself. We kept our eyes resolutely from the porthole window, which was filled at one moment with green heaving sea and the next by steel grey sky. We tried not to focus on Edith's dressing gown as it swung like a pendulum on the cabin door and we turned in loathing from our friend Micky who came down after every meal to tell us what she had eaten.

But all that was now over. We had had a few days of glorious sunshine and calm sea. Once the queasiness of my stomach had settled, I was in my element, enjoying for the first time in my life, or so it seemed, freedom to do as I liked. There was no one to question this freedom save Uncle Welch who tried each morning to pin us down to language study. I could take books from the library and read for hours, with nobody to scold me or give me something to do. As for the meals, after the Spartan diet of College, they were fantastic.

'Are you not enjoying the voyage?' I asked Edith wistfully. 'Not really, I'll be glad to get to India and start work.' I remember looking away from her and staring at the rapidly disappearing white walls of Tangier and feeling guilty again. Was I so different from the other missionary candidates? Were all of them straining at the leash to get to the work God had called them to, looking on the sea voyage as a waste of time, not as a pleasure to be enjoyed? Or could there be others like myself, candidates who had hidden their reluctance and their fears behind starry eyes and fervent valedictory testimonies?

I knew in that moment why I didn't want the voyage to end. It wasn't because I was enjoying the voyage so much. After all, life on board ship was not always pleasant. There was the attitude of fellow passengers, for instance, on finding that we did not join in certain activities – first bewilderment, then on the part of some, resentment, hostility or contempt. And I had always longed passionately to be liked by everybody. No, it was because this was an interlude, a break before I was thrown into the unknown future. I was living completely in the present as in a happy dream, disturbed very little either by homesickness for the past life or fear of the future.

'I'm not fit to be a missionary,' I said, suddenly miserable. 'I don't know why God called me.'

I caught a look of concern on Edith's face and grinned. 'It's all right,' I said. 'I'm not repenting my call. I'm just a bit frightened.'

'Of what? Snakes and tigers? Or having to live hard?'

'Of course not!' I declared vehemently, answering the last question. 'I wouldn't care if I had to live in a mud hut and eat off a banana leaf. I don't know what I'm afraid of. Perhaps it is because I don't know what is ahead of me. Suppose I don't like the people I live with or worse still, suppose they don't like me? I would be miserable and I can't bear not to be happy.'

'That was obvious this morning.' said Edith sarcastically, 'by the way you treated your poor book.'

Someone had left the book *Streams in the Desert* on my bunk in Liverpool. I had been reading it each morning but on this particular day, becoming suspicious, I had turned over more pages and then had flung it across the cabin. Now I had the grace to blush.

'That was because I found it was one continuous hymn of praise to sorrow and suffering. It insisted that the only way God can help us grow spiritually is by allowing us to suffer. And I don't believe it. I think if we pray and read the Bible and always obey at once when God speaks to us, we shall grow without it. It's the disobedient children who have to be made to suffer, isn't it?'

Tangier was now out of sight. People had drifted away from the rail and we were alone, gazing at the sea on which myriad stars twinkled as the sun caught the wavelets.

Edith said: 'I wonder how you came to offer yourself for the foreign field when you are so afraid of being unhappy or unsafe?'

10

CHAPTER TWO

New Life in Christ

Edith's question was not an easy one to answer, as she herself must have known. Many young Christians who long to know the will of God for their lives ask the same question.

'How can you be sure that God wants you to offer for foreign service?' they say.

The missionary candidate, setting out for the first time, can only reply: 'I don't know how I know. But I'm sure God wants me to go, and I must go.'

But later on the candidate-become-missionary (or minister or artist or anyone who has left all to follow the urge) realises that, all his life, events and circumstances have been leading up to, and preparing him for the critical moment of decision and commitment.

So although I had intended to record only the events of my forty-two years in India, the lessons God taught me, the miracles He performed for us, I must go back beyond 1930 when I sailed from Liverpool, and from among the welter of childhood and adolescent memories that have rushed upon me, try to record those that have a bearing on the 'Call', circumstances which I believe God Himself engineered.

If other people's prayers have anything to do with it, and I believe they have, the answer to Edith's question goes back to the time before I was born when my mother prayed that I might become a preacher. She must have been under the influence of Gypsy Smith at the time for she meant to call me Rodney after him. There was no thought in her mind that I might be a girl; both sides of the family had produced only boys. Her half-sister, my aunt Cecily, had already seven lusty sons and my father had been one of five boys. When she saw that she had a baby daughter, she forgot her prayer, women preachers being rare in those days. She would certainly not have wanted to see me preaching to village women at the other side of the world. But the prayer had been made and God was going to answer it in His own way.

An elderly woman called Annie also had something to do with it. She had always loved me and, being convinced that God had a great work for me to do, she had prayed for me every day for years. Then one Saturday evening during a Sunday School party she caught a glimpse of me dancing the Maxina with a friend across the floor of the cellar where we were supposed to be washing up. Fearful that I had set my feet on the slippery path to a life of worldly pleasure, she went home and spent the night in prayer for me – with tears. This is the sort of prayer God delights to answer in such a way that the heart is lifted and faith strengthened. I believe that when God is about to do something wonderful He puts the desire for this thing on the hearts of one or more of His praying people like a burden. They pray, and the thing happens. It was so with Annie's prayer. The next day, something happened to me that changed the whole course of my life.

It was 1921 and I was fifteen. Evening service over, as my friend and I were walking along Fishergate, the main street of our town, two pleasant-faced young women approached us; they asked us if we were going anywhere in particular. Not being the sort to lie easily I said we were not and before we realised what was happening we found ourselves in the brilliantly lit hall of the YWCA. We had been 'fished' in!

I have no happy recollections of the meeting. The speaker talked on interminably while my friend kept up her fiercely whispered demands that we get up and go. But at last the meeting was over and we were at the door, promising to return for the social evening on the Thursday, a promise we had no intention of keeping. Nevertheless, we were there.

'We almost didn't come,' I confided to a girl called Lily R. as we sat drinking tea after two hours of hilarious games. 'After we left on Sunday we remembered that we were to spend the evening with a friend (actually an ex-teacher and our latest crush). We wouldn't have missed that for worlds, but she caught a cold and wrote asking us to postpone our visit.'

'That was God working,' said Lily R. solemnly. 'He meant you to come here.'

'Do you think so?' I said. It was a new thought to me that God should be interested in how I spent an evening. I must have heard many times that He is concerned with every detail of our lives but it was a different matter to be told so by an attractive seventeen-year-old with doggy brown eyes and a thick braid of fair hair tied top and bottom with huge flapper bows.

'I'm sure of it!' she replied. She had a curious way of emphasizing certain words as she spoke then smiling enchantingly as she watched the effect of what she had said. 'I know; I feel it in my heart that you two are fish that are going to stay.'

I saw later how important that evening had been. Had we not returned then we would not have given the place another thought. Nothing had attracted us on the Sunday, but now we found ourselves among the jolliest crowd of girls we had ever met. Their exuberant joy, their warm acceptance of us, the wholesomeness of their conversation, and their natural way of referring to the Lord made a profound impression on me. God could not have found a more suitable 'net' in which to catch and hold me.

We returned happily on the Saturday, prepared to endure a long unfamiliar prayer meeting for the delight that would precede it, a walk with our new friends, returning to the rooms to eat the sandwiches we had brought with us. And the following Sunday we knelt and responded to the invitation to receive the Lord Jesus Christ into our hearts and lives.

I ought to have heard and responded to this invitation long ago for I had been brought up in an atmosphere of Christian worship and service. Though basically a member of the Anglican Church I had spent my earliest years in the Methodist tradition, singing the great Methodist hymns with their emphasis on the new birth, and yearly at the Sunday School Anniversary services I had heard some of the great Methodist preachers – Thomas Waugh, Samuel Chadwick and others. Why had I not found the invitation so real, so personal? I believe it was because it was put to me in ordinary conversation by girls of my own age and because, watching them, I had realised that, Christian though I considered myself to be, I lacked something that marked them.

'Just ask Him to come in, and He will,' said Lily R.

I believe He came into my life that day. He came at the right time, offering me an alternative to the sort of future to which I was heading and which would never have satisfied me.

The new way of life satisfied me completely. I took to it like the proverbial duck to water, accepting without complaint the taboos and restrictions of the group. And in those days taboos for young Christians were many. There was to be no cinema-going (but I hadn't time for that now!); no make-up at all (I had not yet experimented with cosmetics, not having money to spend on them!); no dancing (that hurt a little!); no bobbed or shingled hair; no dating with boys and definitely no artificial silk stockings, that most exciting, shocking addition to female garb recently become available to the poorest. They shocked because they were flesh coloured, so conspicuous since hemlines had risen above the knees, and they were exciting because they promised an end

12

to the ugly black, brown or grey woollen or lisle-thread monstrosities we had endured until now. We knew that the daintier species would come our way once they had ceased to be a spectacle and become part of the everyday scene.

'What miserable, spineless creatures you must have been,' I can hear some present-day teenager exclaim, 'to allow yourselves to be so shackled by older people's stuffy notions.'

But we did not feel shackled. Our generation had, of course, been trained to conform, to respect the opinion of our elders and betters, to accept their standards of right and wrong, their notions of what was seemly and what was not. The post-war years were now offering an escape from this spirit of obedience and many young people were throwing off the old restraints and defying parental control. But although I had been prepared to try my wings, so to speak, to risk shocking my parents in order to be what we now call 'with it', it was almost with a sense of relief that I found myself one of a group who did not feel obliged to be 'with it'. I could be wonderfully happy and fulfilled without hurting my parents or alienating older friends. I was certainly not miserable. Life seemed good to me during those early years after my conversion. I count them among the happiest of my life.

Perhaps my new friends and I found it comparatively easy to conform because we respected the one who set the standard of our dress and behaviour. Our secretary was worthy of our submission and we had the sense to recognise the worthiness. There is nothing degrading about such submission as Oswald Chambers points out in his book – *My Utmost for His Highest.* We give it to Christ. Even in the present permissive age when restrictions are not tolerated and authority is a suspicious word, young Christians come to a full submission to Christ as Lord as well as Saviour because the more fully they know Him the more worthy they find Him.

Our submission was much the same. We didn't keep our long hair for instance; because certain preachers were thundering from the pulpits – if a woman be shorn, let her be shaven – but because our Miss Bear considered the shingled head not only unscriptural but ugly and unwomanly. The more stylish among us, reluctant to be thought old-fashioned or dowdy, coiled our hair over our ears in 'headphones' and so achieved the current line. It was not from some sentimental emotion that we conformed to her standards; there was no question of our having a teenage 'crush' on her, there was no familiarity in the relationship between us. As we grew older, we came to love her greatly but during our teenage years we were moved simply by respect tinged with awe. We might joke about her in her absence, calling her Mother Bear, but in her presence all our flippancy fell away and we allowed her to mould our lives. Sitting around the tea table on Saturday afternoons after a shopping expedition with our particular cronies or a walk in the park where the green lawns sloped down to the River Ribble, we would enjoy the sandwiches we had brought with us and the hot tea dispensed by Marian, the smiling maid, at two pence per head. And we would listen to Miss Bear.

She would share items of interest from the newspapers or some new truth she had discovered during her quiet time with God. Or she would draw us out to tell of what we had seen in the park, an unrecognised bird, and the newest flower to open, the haze of green appearing on the hedges, the colours of the sunset, and she could so easily make a parable of what we had seen. Listening, our town-bred personalities expanded. She taught us to use our eyes and our ears and our minds, to meditate on everything that is beautiful and good and praiseworthy. Looking back, I cannot see that we were in any way the losers for our submission.

13

Perhaps what was most important of all for my future, Miss Bear gave to me a constant reminder of the needs of what we now call – the third world; a constant reminder of the Lord's final command to His people to go into all the world and preach the Gospel. There had been no similar emphasis in the place of worship I had attended all my life. As far as I remember, there had been no call to young people to dedicate themselves for a life of service abroad. It was not a mission-orientated church.

Nevertheless it had its own disciplinary influence on my character so perhaps I should say something about it at this point especially as I believe it was perhaps the last of its kind in England. Mill Hill could not be called a church or chapel or even a mission hall. It had been one of the original Ragged Schools, which had flourished all over England during the 19th century, begun by Robert Raikes and encouraged by Lord Shaftesbury. Here children of the very poor were daily brought in from the cold, given a hot meal and taught to read and write. The need for such day schools ceased with the introduction of free, compulsory education but in my town benevolent people still gathered the children for Sunday School. My Father joined this devoted band in 1890 when he became engaged to my Mother who was already involved.

The Board of Guardians, made up of influential men of the town, continued to supervise the affairs of the school. The most active of these were the Toulmins, a well-known Lancashire family, owners of the *Lancashire Daily Post*. Mr George and Mr Jock supervised the morning and afternoon sessions of Sunday School until after the 1st World War when my Father was appointed to the Board and joined them as Superintendent. He and Mr Jock made a splendid pair when leading the opening and closing sessions. Both were bass singers and, one on the platform and the other walking round the hall, they led the singing lustily, chins tucked behind their high collars. They were good friends and would walk together part of the way towards my home. Wearing bowler hats and immaculate suits and carrying canes, they drew people's attention for they were both over six feet tall, an unusual sight in a county where men tend to be short and stocky.

The children who attended the school were not the ragged children of the old days but they came from the same streets and were poor enough. Some of them were indeed ragged, ill-fed, unkempt and often dirty. Moving amongst them as a child it never crossed my mind that they could be as desperate and as pitiable as the children of the London slums whose harrowing stories we were hearing every day and about whom I read in every Sunday School prize I received. For this was the era of the Temperance Reform Movement, the fervent Band of Hope meeting (the Teetotal Movement had its foundation in Preston) and the approved Sunday reading for children was from books such as *A Peep Behind the Scenes* and *Alone in London*.

While I wept at times for the children of London's East End who sat cold and hungry on the steps of the Public House waiting for Father to come out with what was left of his wages, I don't remember feeling the same pity for the children of our school. I took them as part of my life. When I was singled out and treated differently I was embarrassed even as a small child in the infant school. The teacher of this class was a formidable old lady, (probably not as old as I imagined her to be) who had around seventy undisciplined children to control and to teach. They sat on a sort of gallery of steps, which started at floor level and reached almost to the ceiling. But there were three of us who were not allowed to sit among them. We were lifted carefully on to a form at the side so that our white needlework dresses with their coloured sashes and our cream cashmere coats might not be soiled. I remember being most unhappy in that class though I could not have

14

put my uneasiness into words. My Mother, busy upstairs with her class of boys, knew nothing of it. I'm not sure what she would have done about it had she known.

When I was thirteen I was given a class of small girls, the youngest in the upper school. I seemed to have managed them pretty well though my greatest difficulty was to find enough material to fill the half hour of lesson time twice a day. Work periods were unknown in those days. There was no writing or drawing with coloured pencils to pass the time; it was straight, solid teaching from the Word. I might have been tempted to tell stories; uplifting ones of course, from sources other than the Bible were it not for my Father's disconcerting habit of patrolling the hall and sometimes taking a seat in some class to hear what was being taught.

By the year 1919 the appearance if not the character of the children had changed. The 1st World War had begun the levelling process. Ready-made clothes were becoming possible to the poorest. From my teacher's chair in the lowest class I welcomed each fresh batch of little girls coming to me from the Infant class and each appeared more cosily, more prettily dressed than the last. But though the children were no longer ragged, nobody was interested in changing the name of the school. Mill Hill Ragged School it remained until it fell under the power of the bulldozer during a modern town-planning scheme.

There were times after my conversion when I found my duties at the school becoming more irksome. In my desire to spend more time with my new friends I could easily have been slack and irresponsible if it had not been for my Father. He had been greatly moved by my conversion having had a similar experience in Salonika and now felt it his duty to see that I lived up to my profession. He believed that a Christian's character should be marked by loyalty, faithfulness and dependability and so he curbed my tendency to think I could skip some of my duties at the school to attend more attractive meetings with my friends. He could not force me, of course, but his disapproval was enough to make me forego the pleasure of listening to some visiting preacher elsewhere. Not that I submitted in silence.

'So I have to miss this marvellous preacher and be bored instead by Mr …?' I would get no further. Mr … might expound the Scriptures in a flat Lancashire voice with not a few dropped Hs (and worse still, Hs put in where they should not have been!) but my father would not have the man of God criticized. What I believe happens in some Christian homes round the lunch table on Sundays, the pulling in pieces of the sermon or criticism of the minister himself, rarely took place in our home, if ever. Although I seem to have inherited from one or the other of my parents a strong critical faculty, I was never allowed to use it to the detriment of someone's character. Nor did my parents criticize others in front of us.

My Father was also a pattern of how a Christian should sit under humble, godly men such as the one I was despising. With one long leg crossed over another he would keep his eyes on the preacher to the very end of the longest, dreariest sermon. To this day, I have to keep my eyes on a speaker even though, because of my deafness or because he is speaking in a foreign language, I am getting but a smattering of what he is saying, so strongly has the fact been impressed upon me that a preacher is not blind to the blank or bored faces in front of him, the nodding heads, the furtive glances at watches and that, whether he is old and experienced or young and nervous, he needs interested and intelligent faces on which to focus and from which to take encouragement.

But because my parents were real and sincere, practising what they preached, I did my best to please them. I was with my class of small girls in Sunday School at 9.30am and 2.30pm each

Sunday, hurrying after the morning session to my church, All Saints, for Morning Worship. I was rarely missing from choir practice, and weekly Bible Class, which my Father led. This faithfulness to duty cost me many a happy hour with my friends, especially during that first winter when two of my evenings were taken up with evening classes.

I was taking a commercial course at the Technical School to prepare myself for a better job than the one I had found for myself in a local mill, a job into which I fitted as well as the proverbial square peg in a round hole. Circumstances had driven me to this. The war had done for me what it had done for thousands of other young people of my age; it had deprived me of higher education. There had seemed to be no prospect of an end to the fighting when in 1917 my headmaster put me in the scholarship class and his chagrin was apparent when on my winning the scholarship my Mother refused to allow me to take advantage of it. What else could she do? My Father had already been four years at the Front and the family finances were touching rock bottom. There was no education grant in those days, no help for books and uniforms. Sadly I watched my better-off friends move to the school I had longed to attend, which I had expected to attend. I would meet them occasionally and feel the hurt again as I saw them dressed in the coveted uniform, the jaunty boater with its blue and white band. It was not until I came to know the Lord as my Saviour and Friend that I found comfort in the thought that the twelve-year-old Jesus had once turned His back upon the doctors in the Temple and what might have been a college education and returned to the carpenter's bench.

One of the good things to come out of my uncongenial job was my friendship with Cissie, a cheery girl with long pigtails and an enchanting, turned-up nose. Cissie found the Saviour during those days, receiving Him into her heart and life, and the fellowship we had was sweet. She later married the verger of her church, a man whom people said as they said of Stephen, that he had the face of an angel. With him she blossomed and matured becoming quite a pillar of her church. Our friendship has stood firm to this day when we are both past the allotted three score years and ten.

The evening class also proved in later years to have been of value. The English teacher, a Welshman called Evans, taught me to appreciate literature in a new way. Although his subject was Commercial English, his delight in poetry and prose broke through every lecture. Sitting in his class, learning the art of précis-writing, proof-reading, how to use words and how to economise in words, I first felt the urge to write. I began with poetry (doggerel, my Father called it), stories in rhyme, which I recited on social occasions. I submitted a poem to the first edition of the Girl Guide magazine and won first prize. I never lost that itch to write and these efforts were preparing me for a special missionary task such as I had never dreamed of and which was to bring fulfilment to my life during some difficult and lonely days.

Nevertheless, trying to fit some happy hours with my friends at the rooms along with this course and my duties at the school was taking its toll on my strength. I was becoming tired and nervy. My Father did not see what was happening and my Mother, who was, after all, the chief sufferer from my over-full schedule, hesitated to interfere. 'That girl is always going off somewhere,' said one of my relatives one evening as I was slipping out of the house. I listened for my Mother's reply for I often felt twinges of conscience over the little help that I gave her. I smiled when the answer came.

'But I know she is safe where she is.'

Perhaps that was something in the 'roaring twenties'.

16

CHAPTER THREE

God Wants You Now

'But I don't want to become a missionary! I've no intention of becoming a missionary; I'm happy where I am.'

We were a small group seated round the huge stove in the hall, warming ourselves before facing the wintry weather outside. We had had a missionary speaker that evening which event had no doubt caused someone to make what was becoming a tiresomely frequent remark about my being the next missionary candidate. And I was giving my usual reply.

Emily turned her dark eyes on me and looked away again. 'Betty is afraid of the sacrifice,' she said.

There was something smug and self-righteous about her, in what she said and the look on her face. I felt my temper rising.

'What about yourself?' I retorted. 'You talk a great deal about the Mission Field but you make no move to go.'

'I haven't had a call,' said Emily loftily.

'Neither have I. It is all of you who are deciding for me and I'm just about tired of it.'

An embarrassed silence fell on the group and I must have flushed to my ears.

'I'm sorry,' I said 'but you make me feel all mixed up and different.'

Miss Grapes, principal of Redcliffe Missionary Training College had brought about this situation. Some months before, she had been paying a visit to our secretary who had been one of her students and was now a close friend. We knew all about this awesome person. Two of our older friends were studying under her at the time and what they told us of life in the college filled me with horror. They, of course, thought it wonderful, but the impression they gave of her was of a frightfully severe person who imposed hard disciplines and whose eyes could look right through yours to your innermost thoughts so I for one intended to keep out of her way.

One evening, I came face to face with her on the stairs. Miss Bear introduced us and while she told something about me, the lady's eyes were searching mine. To my surprise I detected a twinkle of amusement.

'This girl will be a missionary one day,' she said, suddenly serious. 'When the time comes, we shall be glad to welcome her to Redcliffe.'

Escaping, I fled to my friends and reported the conversation with some ill-bred mimicry and a good deal of giggling. The significance of what she said was lost in my excitement at being singled out in this way. But I was to repent bitterly of having told anyone of the interview. The notion that I was to be the next missionary candidate fixed itself firmly in the minds of all my friends. At first I simply laughed at the suggestion but after a while I began to feel irritated by it, even resentful. It was so easy for them, I thought, to be planning the disruption of my future when they themselves had no such foreboding.

I aired my grievances before Miss Bear one day. I was spending the afternoon with her in her room, which overlooked Fishergate, the main street of our town. It was a quiet room. Traffic was thinner in the twenties than it is now, only the occasional clanging of a tram or the clip-clop of horses' hooves on the stone sets of the road disturbed the silence.

'Even my Father can't forget it,' I said. 'He says "Mary Slessor!" in a sarcastic tone of voice whenever I have to be reprimanded for something I've done or left undone. Miss Bear smiled. 'He's probably dismayed at the thought that Miss Grapes might be a true prophet and they will lose you. You'll just have to see to it that you do nothing to earn a reprimand! I watched her as she poured the tea and suddenly wondered why I had not noticed before how beautiful she was. I had seen only the penetrating quality of her deep-set grey eyes, their power to quell with a look, to make one feel gauche or vulgar or just a plain worm. I hadn't noticed the laughter lines at the corners, the high cheek bones or the way her hair grew back in a lovely line from her wide, calm brow. Now I saw how beautifully formed her mouth was – wide and generous — which was as well for her since she often insisted that while we were not responsible for our other features, we each had the making of our own mouths.

I think of her still when I occasionally meet an elderly lady whose mouth has set in a hard, thin, obstinate line, or in a petulant droop, or is pursed in perpetual disapproval. And since my own facial muscles have begun to slacken I have at times scanned my drooping mouth in the mirror with apprehension.

Having settled me with a cup of tea and a cake, Miss Bear leaned back and said: 'Now, let me hear what is really troubling you.'

I thought for a moment, then I replied: 'If God should want me to go abroad, how shall I know that it is He calling me and not just other people's opinions pressing on me? It's what God says to me that matters, isn't it.'

'Yes, darling, but perhaps you are not listening very hard. Perhaps God still has to speak to you through other people. Sometimes it is the only way He can get a word to us.'

I saw what she meant and I nodded. She thought I wasn't taking enough time to listen to God. Of course, I wasn't. My days were far too full, all my spare time taken up with meetings of some sort. I had already begun to realize that I was doing too much. I was tired and jaded yet I didn't seem to be able to cut down my activities. I seemed to have made myself indispensable.

'When God wanted Paul and Barnabas to go out as missionaries, He told the elders of the Antioch Church; and they sent the two out. It is surely the ideal way for a missionary to go out; knowing that her church or group are convinced that she is God's choice and so they send her and will support her.'

'Then you think the folk are right about me?'

'I wouldn't discount it,' she replied. 'I would think it over very seriously. When you get to the mission field (so she thought the same!) you will be a much more easily handled candidate if you have accepted the fact that your Board or Field Council could possibly know the Lord's will for you better than you know yourself.'

I left the room with mixed feelings. The interview had not done for me what I had hoped it would. I had wanted Miss Bear to tell me to take no notice of what other people were saying and that it was ridiculous of them to put so much meaning into what Miss Grapes had said, as if she were a prophet, that this was an intimate matter between me and God. But she hadn't said it.

But the talk had opened my eyes to one thing. There was no intimate matter between me and God. I had no intimate relationship with Him at all. I hadn't allowed time for such a fellowship to develop. I loved Him. I loved His word. I loved singing about Him and to Him. But I didn't know

Him. I wasn't really in touch with Him.

In the days that followed, I found that much of the exuberance, the buoyancy, had gone from my happiness. It wasn't because of the missionary problem; I could forget that most of the time, but because I saw that I was a failure as a Christian. I wasn't real. I was giving a show of spirituality that didn't exist in my inner life. It wasn't that I was trying to impress people – I loathed anything affected. Yet people were apparently impressed, endowing me with something I felt I didn't have. I was, I felt, a bit of a sham.

I tried to remedy this. I gave more time to prayer, or tried to do so, and began to study the Bible. I had been feeding my soul with snippets from *Daily Light* and other devotional books but now I tried to find some deep truths for myself. I wasn't very successful for I needed to get up earlier in the morning and I seemed to have no will power for that. So I was beginning to feel depressed when one Saturday evening I believed I had found the answer.

I was in a prayer meeting. The leader of it was young and enthusiastic and she brought a message that was startling. It was the Keswick message of the power of the Indwelling Christ. This could not have been new teaching to me. I had invited the Lord Jesus Christ into my heart and life some years before and I had believed that He had entered. But I had accepted this great mystery of God in a vague sort of way; it hadn't meant much to me. Now it came to me with exhilarating clarity. Christ by His Spirit was actually living in me, the power at the centre of my life. All I needed to do was to commit myself utterly to Him, to keep nothing back. Given full control, there was no limit to what He could do. He could make me all that He wanted me to be – all that I longed to be.

As I listened I became more and more aware of what I had been missing. The speaker, a student from one of the missionary colleges and not much older than myself, was revealing with every sentence the fullness of the life she was living, her joy in the Lord, her close fellowship with Him, her fruitful prayer life. My own spiritual life was being revealed to me for the shallow thing it was and my exhilaration faded away.

When we knelt to pray I buried my face in my hands and felt the tears trickling through my fingers. At that moment I was experiencing what I had not known before – a real repentance toward God. I was sorry that for so long I had left Him out of the centre of my life, my thoughts and my ambitions, being concerned with my own happiness, with myself. I had been in love with the Christian way of life but had known little of warm, personal love for my Saviour. I had not carefully sought a regular, personal contact with Him. Now I was pouring out my sorrow for all which for the first time I was seeing as sin; 'sin of not loving Thee, sin of not trusting Thee, infinite sin'.

As I prayed for forgiveness and cleansing, I felt quietened, the inconsequential thoughts that were always surging in and out of my over-active mind were banished. I was alone with the Lord.

As we were rising for the final hymn, I longed for this sense of being alone with Him to remain. I wanted to walk home by myself, not with the girls whose company I had always welcomed for the long walk to my home at the other side of the town. (No buses plied the streets in the twenties; if one didn't live on a tram route one walked!) I put down my hymn book and slipped from the room.

Walking alone through the dark and silent streets I committed myself utterly to Christ to do what He would in me and through me. A great weight was lifted from my spirit; I felt as if I walked on air. The exhilaration returned. I began to sing softly:

"I'll go where you want me to go, dear Lord,
Over desert or mountain or sea."
I'll say what you want me to say, dear Lord,
I'll be what you want me to be.

I meant it too, for it seemed to me that life was now going to be wonderful and fine.

I cannot remember whether or not I had been given the notion that from now on I was going to have complete victory in my Christian life – victory over the things that shamed me, my failures and my weaknesses. I certainly thought that I was never going to lose my temper again or find an untruth slipping from my lips. I must have thought that I was starting on a joyride to Heaven, sitting back at ease while the Lord guarded my mind and my lips. I was to find quite soon that God does not work in that way.

Nevertheless, I had grasped a great truth, namely that if there would be any change in me, any deepening of my spiritual life, any growth in grace and knowledge, any bringing forth of fruit in service, it would be all the Lord's doing. I, by myself, had failed. What my part was to be I would find out step by step. At the moment I knew only that I was to learn to love the Lord with all my heart and soul and mind and strength, to keep Him first in my life and thoughts, I must renew my efforts to find time each day to be quiet in His presence, to keep in touch with Him, to trust Him and obey Him whatever He might say to me.

From that evening, my life took a different turn. Evidence of this I find in an early diary. This is a thick notebook I had bought with some hope of becoming another Anne of Green Gables and in which I recorded my intimate thoughts and desires. These were now changing. For instance, there were evidences that I was no longer frantically searching for enough material to fill the half hours of my Sunday School lessons. I was praying more about them. Soon I could record a short list of girls who had been converted.

Then about that time my Father asked me to take over the weekly Bible class. The number of young people attending far outnumbered the older ones and they were happy to have the nature of the meeting changed. We called ourselves Young Seekers. We explored the Bible together and several young people found new life in Christ.

Most important of all, the urge to offer myself for foreign service grew stronger and stronger until I could resist it no longer. But I must be sure that it was the Lord calling me. I would put out a 'fleece'. I remembered that a young man from China was to speak at our meeting on the Saturday evening. I knew him by sight, knew him as one knows other Christians in the town, but because he had become a missionary I would know him better than he knew me. Nevertheless I asked the Lord to let him speak to me personally about the mission field if indeed I was to go. To my dismay he didn't turn up. I had been almost sick with apprehension before the meeting but now I didn't know what to do.

Next morning, walking home from church alone, cutting up a short street to the park I had to cross, I saw him. He was crossing the street at the top. He looked down and saw me and waited for me. We walked but a few yards along the park avenue when he said: 'What are you going to do with you life? Have you ever thought of the mission field?'

I told him about my 'fleece' and he threw up his hat in the air and shouted 'hallelujah'!

When I told Miss Bear of this wonderful miracle she said: 'How kind God is! So now you are convinced that this is what God wants you to do?'

I nodded. 'I think I have been expecting it all along but kept hoping I was mistaken. It's so definitely not what I would have chosen for myself. I'm still frightened of taking the step but I'm more frightened of being out of the will of God for my life. I think of His will as a sort of circle; if I'm inside that circle, nothing can touch me but what He allows. It seems to me that His will is the safest place on earth! I'm much more afraid of being out of it than going to India or China.'

Yet some time was to pass before I made a move. My mother scalded her feet badly and I had to nurse her and keep house for weeks. Then I was not well. But at the end of a year I knew suddenly that the time had come to do something about the call, but what?

That week our Young Seekers meeting had been postponed because of some visiting preacher so I was free to stay at home. After my parents had left the house I knelt with my face in my hands and said: 'Lord, if You'll go with me – if You will assure me now that You will go with me, I'll go.'

I had opened my Bible at random, ready for use when needed. It lay open at Exodus 3 and as I lifted my head the words almost leapt at me from the page – *Certainly I will be with thee.*

Awed I whispered: When, Lord? Do you want me to make a move now? How shall I begin? Whom shall I approach?

When my parents returned I had had no further word. 'You missed a great meeting,' my father said. 'The speaker was from China. He made a terrific impression. We've all ordered the magazine and some took boxes.'

I looked at the magazine he had thrown on the table. It was the organ of The Bible Churchman's Missionary Society, the mission, which had caught my imagination more than any other. I opened the magazine – it was a specimen copy and the usual leaflets fell out. Under my startled gaze a card lay on the table displaying in bold capitals: GOD WANTS YOU NOW.

I shall not forget the day I was interviewed by three prominent members of this mission. In Bolton I faced first of all the awe-inspiring Rev. Percy Stott who looked at me searchingly across the desk and barked, 'How many people have you led to the Lord?' The second man seemed sorry for me and answered most of his questions himself. Then I went on to Manchester to meet a lady whose name I have forgotten. She was not well that day and the maid showed me into her bedroom. As I crossed the floor she cried, 'Oh, my dear! How can your Mother bear to let you go?'

With the favourable (as they must have been) reports of three very different people I was accepted for training. One evening in September of that year, 1928, my friends gathered to wish me Godspeed as I was about to enter Mount Hermon Bible College. The vicar of All Saints Church, the Rev. E.M. Benson, gave the address and his text was from Exodus 3, verse 12 - *Certainly I will be with thee.*

Mount Hermon Bible College

'You're wanted in the principal's office, Faz. (my surname was Fazackerly). You'd better hurry, she looks serious!' My fellow students grinned cheerfully at me before disappearing.

I smoothed my hair and scanned my white collar in the mirror. It was a bit grubby at the neck but I couldn't do anything about that now. I braced my shoulders and made my way to the study. I knew I had asked for this summons, had half expected it, but not so soon. The visiting speaker could hardly be out of sight. Surely it wasn't such a faux pas that I had made in her meeting?

She was a missionary from India and regaled us with stories of her experience when she first visited an Indian Zenana. The women folk had asked her senior colleague the usual questions about her. How old was she, the new one? Was she married? Why was her hair that colour? Why was she not married?

An older woman of the Zenana had answered the final question before her colleague could reply. 'The English don't need to get married; they can always get a man.' I grinned, not seeing at first the significance of what the woman had said. I thought our speaker was trying to be funny! I glanced at the principal who was sitting facing us. She was looking hard at me – and she was not smiling.

I tapped on the study door, more excited than nervous. I was going to have a 'private interview' with the principal for whom I already had a great admiration. Miss Crocker was in her first year at Mount Hermon and must have been very young at the time. She was far removed from the image I had had of a Bible college principal - someone elderly, severe, gimlet-eyed and quite terrifying. Miss Crocker was young and fun-loving and adorable. Full of life and vigour she could, for instance, knock us all out for six when she joined us on the Podox field, hitting the ball in all directions. But nobody took advantage of her youth or friendly ways. She had a natural dignity of bearing, a superb carriage, and what is more, we all had a healthy regard for those smiling hazel eyes which seemed to miss nothing.

Sitting on the edge of a chair, I found those eyes resting on me with an expression I couldn't read. She didn't speak for a few moments and I was suddenly aware of my grubby collar. Or perhaps I had a spot on my navy blue dress. I looked away toward the window. Heads topped by the ridiculous, deaconess-type bonnets bobbed along the hedge in twos and threes. The others were going for a walk without me. Beyond them, the trees that lined the edge of Streatham Common had not yet lost their leaves. A copper beech glowed golden in the late afternoon sunshine. It was a scene that had delighted my town-bred soul every day since my arrival. The principal's first words brought my eyes back to her with a jerk.

'I want you to tell me what you know of the facts of life.'

I knew a moment of panic. I thought: oh, she thinks I am a little innocent, not safe out! She is feeling she must enlighten me before she allows me to go to some wicked place abroad. But she is nervous! I must head her off!

'Do you mean the hard knocks of life, Miss Crocker?' I asked brightly, 'Because I haven't had any.'

A small smile twitched at the corner of her mouth and her eyes twinkled. I cannot remember how she answered but I know that I was soon pouring out my life story, encouraged by her questions. At length she said.

'Are you happy now that you are in college?'

I assured her that I was thoroughly enjoying life. 'I didn't want to come at first,' I added. 'I prayed that the Board wouldn't send me here.'

'Did you? Why?'

'It was the uniform,' I said, and had the grace to blush. 'A deaconess in our town wore it and I thought it horribly ugly. I didn't like her much either, and she had been a student here. But I'm glad now that God didn't answer my prayer.'

This was true. I wasn't finding training the nightmare I had expected it to be. For one thing, I found myself once more among people. A lot of people. The Lord's happy people. That was enough to counteract for me any problem or irksome discipline, for whatever I may have lacked as a Christian I had this – I loved the brethren!

I found out that being a BCMS candidate carried with it extra joys. Once a month we were excused College Prayer Meeting, going up to the city to attend the Mission's monthly gathering in Church House, Westminster. It was a half day of freedom the others envied us of. After the meeting a lady whose name I have forgotten invariably slipped a half crown into Edith's hand to pay for our teas. Sometimes Mr Titterton of the London Jews' Society, who lectured us on Comparative Religions, would do the same with me. With five shillings* the six of us could regale ourselves with tea and toast at Lyons and pay our fares back to College.

Then we were invited once a month to take tea and supper with Admiral and Lady Stileman at Upper Norwood. My Sunday School class was in Mitcham so I would arrive for tea hot and tired after cycling or pushing my bike to the top of Beulah Hill. But what a tea there was and what a jolly crowd we were, six of us and the same number of fellows from the Missionary Training Colony at Norwood, sitting round the table (no balancing teacups and dropping crumbs of cake!) laughing uproariously at the Admiral's jokes. After tea and before the Colony fellows left we would gather round the piano to sing hymns, cheering the Admiral on when he could be persuaded to sing — Master, the tempest is raging — in his deep booming voice.

College life had its irksome discipline, of course. I disliked tea without sugar, for instance, and having to clear one's plate completely spoiled many dinner hours for me though I generally managed to hide the bits of fat under my fork. The household chores dismayed me at first because of the limited time allowed but I soon learned to clean out a room thoroughly in half an hour. It took a good many embarrassing trips to the Sister's room to claim my belongings which had been confiscated before I saw the advantages of having a place for everything and keeping it there. I even accepted the uniform after a while. In fact, I became quite fond of my wee deaconess bonnet, secretly thinking I looked quite fetching in it!

I revelled in the lectures and was never bored by the hours set apart for study, but there was one part of the curriculum I never enjoyed.

'I enjoy everything,' I said now to Miss Crocker, 'except Monday afternoon. I hate visiting.'

'Dear me! And what will you do when you are in India or China and your life is made up of visiting? You are going out as an evangelist, you know!'

I shuddered. 'Yes, but perhaps it won't be the same out there. People won't resent me as the

---

* *equivalent to 25p*

23

women in Peckham do. They will want me. I wouldn't mind visiting so much if there were two of us. Why do I have to go alone, Miss Crocker? And some of the girls work with a church. They have a nice chat with the minister or the deaconess over a cup of tea – that's three-quarter's of an hour gone – and then they go out with a list of names. They can say: 'Good afternoon, Mrs So-and so. I've come from St. Mark's.' And the lady says: 'Oh, yes. Come in. I'm just making a cup of tea.' And that's another half hour of visiting gone. I have to go straight into it, house to house, knocking at closed doors and feeling sick because I don't know what I shall say when the door opens. Sometimes it is slammed in my face. I can't blame the women for getting mad with me. I feel it is – is impertinent, a young girl like me thinking I have anything to give these women who know so much more of life.'

I saw a look on Miss Crocker's face which was becoming a familiar one to me. When she spoke there was the bracing quality in her voice and not a little sarcasm. 'Are you quite finished?' she asked. 'If you thought less about your own feelings and more about the Word of Life which you have and which they need, you would go less reluctantly.'

There is no record in my diary of our ever reaching the subject of the facts of life. But there was one other occasion when I bared my soul to her. I had been kept in bed for a few days and had had ample solitude in which to think about myself and my spiritual progress. I had come to the conclusion that I was a bigger failure as a Christian now than before I came to the college.

'I'm discouraged, Miss Crocker,' I said to her one afternoon as she sat on the side of my bed. 'I have wrong thoughts that I can't control; wrong reactions to things.'

'Such as?'

'I'm getting up against Olive. (Olive was the 'captain' of my bedroom and our two personalities were quite incompatible). I resent being bossed by her because I don't think she cares at all about us, what we do or what we say. Then I find myself becoming resentful because I'm never asked to play the organ for the Friday meeting. And I'm having to fight my wrong feelings since you asked Emily to form a choir. You see, these are the things I would have been doing at home. It's jealousy, I know, but I've never had to fight it like this before.'

'Perhaps you've never had cause to be jealous before,' she said rather tartly. 'You are beginning to find out now that you are not the only one with talents.' Then she smiled at me. 'This is one of the reasons why you are here, you know, to be exposed to circumstances that will open your eyes to see yourself as you really are, revelations better faced before you get to the mission field. It is a good thing, dear, to find out that there is more in you for the Lord to deal with than your hasty temper and rather impertinent tongue.'

I stared at her in amazement. How did she know that I had considered these my only sins?

'People will tell you, with a knowing smile, that your greatest problem out there will be your fellow missionaries. It is considered by some to be the smart thing to say to a candidate. But it will be much better for the peace of some mission station if you learn now that your greatest problem is yourself, if you find now that you are not as liveable with as you thought you were. It may be a shattering experience to find that you are touchy, you are prone to jealousy, you react badly to other people's moods, that you can't bear to be criticized or ordered about, a discovery best made here where pressures are not so great. You won't be so liable to sulk or to blame the other person when your natures prove to be incompatible.'

In many parts of the world today there are hundreds of women who remember Miss Crocker with love and gratitude and perhaps each one remembers her for a different reason. I, looking back over fifty years, see her as an intensely practical person, a real person. She despised all cant and superficial piety. She exposed religious clichés, made us think over and think through every statement we made. Faithfully she exposed our faults and weaknesses, stripping from us any false notions we might be harbouring about ourselves.

I am not minimising the importance she laid on every other aspect of missionary training but I think she bent each one to obtain the same objective, namely, that we should become real and sincere, fully equipped to face whatever we might meet on the mission field. Her Bible studies, for instance, gave us the whole sweep from Genesis to Revelations, revealing the purpose of God running like a shining thread throughout and linking book with book, casting every doubt from our minds of this being the inspired word of God.

But even these lectures rarely ended without a practical application, a penetrating word that made some of us squirm and others to wonder if the principal could be gifted with second sight! A great love grew between Miss Crocker and me, yet in her faithfulness she never spared me. If I finally went to India with anything left of my smug self-complacency, it surely was not her fault.

CHAPTER FIVE

Saugor

Fifth of November and I awoke to a stifling heat. Not a breath of air was coming through the porthole and there was a strange silence in the cabin. Some sound that had been with us for three weeks was not there; the throbbing of the engines had ceased. We had docked in the night.

So there was no dim, romantic shoreline to fill us with ecstasy as there had been for the girl Ada. We had no exciting glimpses of the Gateway of India across sparkling, blue water. The first sight of our new land came to us as we peered through the porthole – the wharf at Bombay, where giant cranes were already dropping with sickening thuds huge bundles of baggage held together in nets.

We spent an exceedingly uncomfortable hour trying to keep sweet and unruffled and out of each other's way as we dressed and finished the packing in the small space and with perspiration running into our eyes and trickling down our backs. Then after breakfast, with everyone looking strange in their shore-going clothes, came the agony of the long wait in the Customs shed, hoping that the officer wouldn't find anything in one's baggage that one had forgotten to declare and that the over-full case might not refuse to shut again once he had turned the contents over.

At last we were out of the docks and on to the streets of Bombay through which we drove, two by two, in ancient victorias, watching fearfully for any signs of rioting; for this was 1930 and even now Mahatma Gandhi was illegally distilling salt on the beaches of Bombay, inciting men to rebellion. When the ancient Jehu driving us began to whip up the horse and yell at the top of his voice, my companion Eileen and I clung to each other in terror. It was his way of dealing with obstinate jay-walkers, but we were not to know that.

Then Victoria station appeared which I can only describe as marble halls. At least it seemed so that day. I remember the vast, marble-floored dining room where fans whirred above our heads, clean white clothes covered the tables and the waiters hovered over us clad in spotlessly white coats and turbans. Alas, these have long disappeared – not the white coats but the spotlessness and the whiteness. We ate a meal of sorts accompanied by spongy bread and buffalo butter which was as white as lard. Then we were in the train, in a large, almost square compartment with padded seats on all four sides, and a bathroom attached. All this for the four of us – Mr and Mrs Welch, Dorothy and myself. Although in those days there was no such convenience as berth reservations, and certainly no 'Europeans only' notice appeared over the door, no one attempted to enter. We were to travel in isolated splendour, visited at every step by obliging waiters from the dining car. We were in British India. We were the Sircar – the Government!

The scene on the platform was fascinating. My chief impression was of hats – a diversity of hats. Not women's, but men's. Predominant were the turbans, the large loosely swathed off-white turbans of the countrymen and the smaller, neater, brightly coloured ones worn by the Sikhs. The red fez of the Muslim worn at every possible angle contrasted vividly with the sober pillbox of the babu* class. The black coal scuttle hats of the Parsees towered above the rest and mingling with them all the white pith helmets of the Anglo-Indian railway officials. It was to take the combined

*clerk

26

influence of the 2nd World War and Independence to change this kaleidoscope of headgear. Because of rising costs, few villagers would be able to afford to wind six yards of cloth around their heads, while some change in the Muslim world was to do away with the red fez overnight. The pill-box was to disappear, its place taken in some cases by the white cotton Gandhi cap, the badge of the Congress party, and for the rest the hatless fashion of the West would prevail. But this was not to be for another fifteen to twenty years.

Leaving the station, our train crawled through the outskirts of Bombay with many stops. Life in the tall apartments which lined the track, their backs to it, was open to our view, for the small balconies outside each room were obviously used as kitchens. A girl in a bright, cerise sari was lighting a Primus stove. I watched her put on a pan of water to boil, then tip some tea into a cup from a paper poke. On the balcony above her a sulky looking girl knitted furiously, and next door to her a man, almost naked, squatted on the floor and rolled out chapattis.

When evening came we were still running through the Western Ghats, sometimes in the shadow of deep gorges, sometimes out on the open plain. The sun cast its golden light over the landscape and the flat topped hills were dark against the glowing sky. I sat at the open window, the sun-soaked breeze warm on my cheeks, and watched a silver sickle of a moon with its attendant star appear in a sky still pale blue. Birds were gathering on the telephone wires, sometimes as many as twenty in a line, chattering, restless, bronze green bee-eaters. And sitting alone, his forked tail swinging as he balanced on the wire, the Black Dronga, the farmer's friend and called by them, as I was to learn afterwards, the Watchman.

It was during this long journey to Saugor that India cast her first spell over me. I awoke the next morning to the tumultuous sounds of an Indian railway station. Sitting up, I felt the grit on my face and stared at my filthy hands and the smuts on my frock. Auntie Welch, her face shining from the application of soap and water, was sitting sideways on the opposite seat, a tray of teas beside her and mounds of toast which she was buttering. Uncle Welch stood outside the door chatting to an Indian gentleman and on the seat at right angles to my own, Dorothy was still storing gently.

'Go and wash your hands; choti hazri* is here,' said Auntie Welch. Her eyes were shining and I knew that she was thrilled to the core to be back again among the dirt and smells and sights of rural India.

It was undoubtedly rural India through which we were passing. The great central plain stretched on either side of us – the jungle, Uncle Welch called it, but to me it seemed more like the wilderness I had imagined the Children of Israel to have crossed, stony ground with short, dry grass, broken by scrub and thorn trees, small gullies and sudden low hills. Now and again that day, we thundered over long bridges spanning immensely wide rivers, many of them showing already dry beds. The villagers threw coins from the windows of the train to appease the god of the river.

So, as evening was once more filling the landscape with a golden light, transforming it to a scene of pastoral peace and beauty, we came to Bina where we were to leave Dorothy. Here we spent the night and my only memory of it is waking to the sound of harsh voices singing: 'Speak Lord, in the stillness while we wait on Thee'. I thought: I'm not waiting on God. I haven't waited on Him for days. I'm too restless, too excited. So many strange things to see. I'll settle when we

---

*little breakfast

27

get to Saugor.

I hadn't as yet felt the need for the assuring, comforting presence of the Lord who had said: "Certainly I will be with thee."

Later that day we chugged into Saugor station to the sound of exploding crackers which the schoolboys had laid on the line to greet us. On the platform I saw four young women, pith-helmeted and wearing unfashionably long dresses. They were the past students of Mount Hermon whom I expected to be living with. I saw my future senior missionary with his wife and two small children, some Indian men in pillbox hats and two women in spotless white saris with blue borders which in this part of the world marked them out as Christian Biblewomen. The schoolboys were standing in a long line, huge grins above khaki or crimson shirts.

The greetings were first of all for the Welches. I hung back, but Gladys Simm was beside me, giving me a welcome. Then she said that which filled me with dismay. 'I'm sorry, but you won't be living with us. You will be in the main bungalow, but we are not far away; you'll be seeing quite a lot of us.'

Then I too was surrounded, being greeted by Europeans and Indians alike. They gave me a heart-warming welcome and two exciting days of parties and visits. I attended an Indian silver wedding celebration and ate curry so hot that the tears ran down my cheeks.

Auntie Welch was a great help to me during those few days. She showed me how to deal with the washerman who to my consternation I had found squatting on my bedroom floor sorting out my very dirty, travel-stained linen. She told me what to do with the canister of boiling water a grinning boy had dumped in my bathroom. From her I learned a few simple sentences to ease my way – how to express my needs to the servant, how to greet people I met in the road. And when she had explained the noises I heard in the night and which sounded like rats skating over the cloth ceiling of my room were only playful squirrels, they did sound less frightening.

On the third evening, I went with my seniors to convey the Welchs to their own station sixty miles away, returning so late and so sleepy I hardly realized that I was now alone with strangers. I was to realize it next morning.

The loud, raucous call of a bird hailing the dawn awoke me. I lay for a few moments listening to the strange sound which was coming apparently from the creeper on the verandah outside my bedroom door. I was reluctant to open my eyes, conscious of a weight somewhere in the region of my chest. I didn't want to face the day. Slowly I opened my eyes and at first could see nothing but the tent-like mosquito curtain of fine white net into which I was securely tucked. Then as the daylight strengthened, the room and its contents became visible.

It was a large room, four-square, with whitewashed walls and a stone-flagged floor. There was a double door in each of the four walls. On my right as I lay in bed was the door of the sitting-room. Facing me, a French window opened on to the verandah and the garden, and behind me was the communicating door between mine and the next bedroom, now empty, and on the left the door into the bathroom. Each door was curtained to give privacy, I supposed, during the hot season when all the doors would be open to allow the breeze to blow right through the house.

Now every object was becoming clearer. I could see my pith helmet, huge and white, hanging on the door to the right. I had bought it as early as Marseille for Uncle Welch didn't trust the sun beyond Cyprus!

Next was my desk with my Hindi books in a neat pile ready for my lesson. My family photo stood next to the books but I dare not look at that, not at this early hour. On the dressing table which was old and shabby and complete with fly-spotted swinging mirror, I could see my new cheval set; my mother had helped me to choose it. Hastily I turned to look at the time. My lovely travelling clock was ticking away on the bedside table; it had been my brother's gift to me...

A sensation of nausea clutched me, making me shudder. Soon it would reach my throat and I could be completely undone. Resolutely I pushed aside the mosquito net and slid out of bed. I shook my slippers before thrusting my feet into them as I had been told to do in case a scorpion had decided to sleep in one of them. Then I went into the bathroom, determined to drown this horrible homesickness in cold water. The bathroom was smaller than the bedroom but still quite large, also whitewashed and stone-floored. The farther corner of the floor had been partitioned off by a lower wall two bricks high to form a well; in this stood a tub such as I had been bathed in as a child. A hole in the outside wall at floor level served as an outlet for the water. I had been told always to see that the brick which stood by it was firmly in place over the hole at night lest a snake get in that way. A large earthenware vessel of water stood to one side of the well with an empty syrup tin for a dipper. A wooden commode adorned one corner and to the right as I entered was a white-painted washstand. A hole in the centre of this allowed the aluminium bowl to sit firmly. One used the dipper to fill the bowl and having washed, one threw the water into the well.

The cold water did nothing to help me. Waves of homesickness surged over me as I dressed. It was the worst bout I had had since leaving home. Slipping into a coat, for the early mornings were chilly, I picked up my Bible and went on to the verandah. For a moment my homesickness retreated as I caught my breath, entranced by the scene before me.

The bungalow was built on the side of a hill. Beyond the narrow strip of garden the ground dropped gently into a valley so wooded that the city which lay below me was completely hidden save for four white minarets of a Muslim mosque thrusting up through the trees. In the distance lay a huge lake, shrouded in mist at this hour, and beyond it rose the jagged Gwalior hills. The landscape was utterly different from what I had expected and I revelled in it.

My delight was short-lived for at this moment my breakfast tray was brought to me. I stared at it in stupefaction. While the Welches had been with us, we had eaten breakfast all together. Even now I could hear the family as they settled round the table further along the verandah, but round a corner out of sight of me. I didn't know it was a common custom among missionaries, apart from families, to have breakfast served in the bedrooms in order to prolong the quiet hour before starting work. I thought my seniors didn't want me with them.

I began to drink my tea in miserable gulps and pushed some of the toast down with difficulty. I don't remember what else was served. I only know that the toast was thick and soft, the bread slightly sour. The buffalo butter, white like lard, was made no more palatable by the pear jam! (I must explain here that I haven't had to eat sour bread and pear jam all my life in India. The pear jam was peculiar to my hostess and she had probably put too much yeast in the bread.)

My tray removed, I opened my Bible and began to read. I have no recollection of the verses I read and my diary for this period is of no help. (I was like the sun-dial — I recorded only the sunny hours!) The words must have been comforting, promising the Lord's help and presence, for I remember realizing that although I had loved the promises all my life, having no doubts about their truth, I was now going to prove by experience whether or not I could trust them. For this very day I could have quoted the words of Job had I known them: 'The thing that I greatly feared has

29

come upon me.'

I had arrived in Saugor at a difficult time. Something had gone wrong on the compound but I, the new recruit, was not to be drawn into it. Perhaps some evil had been exposed, some filthy immorality among the schoolboys or treachery among the teachers. Perhaps there had been the moral collapse of a well-loved and respected preacher. These things happen. Or it could have been that two incompatible personalities had come to a head-on clash, disrupting the fellowship. Whatever it was, I was to be sheltered from the knowledge of it.

Sitting outside my bedroom door with my study books I would hear voices. The four girls would appear round the side of the house and go into the office. One day there were missionaries from another station. One and another would catch sight of me and throw a vague smile in my direction but their eyes would remain troubled, not really focusing on me. They meant to be kind. They wanted to save me from early disillusionment, from what we nowadays would call cultural shock, but their kindness only added to my loneliness. I could have stood the impact of any amount of cultural shock, however sudden and devastating, better than this loving conspiracy to shelter me but which only shut me out. I was not weeping or praying or pleading with the rest of them. They left me with only myself to weep for.

Throughout this period, mercifully short, I found an almost miraculous power in the words of Scripture to comfort. It was amazing the way my daily readings held just the right word, or my Bible would fall open at some appropriate place. As soon as I began to read, the lump in my throat began to disappear, the smart of tears behind my eyes cool.

Oh, I know that there is something immature, something naïve in this method of seeking reassurance, this plucking out of comforting texts from the daily reading as we used to pluck them out of the promise-box, discarding the ones that didn't appeal to us and fishing for another! It is not only immature but can be dangerous. There can be times when we are quite blind to the fact that we ourselves are quite responsible for our present misery, that we have brought it on by our own self-centredness, our indifference to the feelings of others, our critical spirit, our sheer failure to be liveable with. To claim then the comforting promises that seem to leap from the page for us – he that toucheth you, toucheth the apple of His eye, for instance, can only pander to our self-pity and may even produce that greatest of all bores – the self-righteous, suffering martyr.

But in times of real desolation, especially when we are young and don't know our way around the Bible too well and have not had much experience of God's sustaining power because we haven't been so tested, then He is infinitely kind. He sends His Word and heals us, no matter the ways in which we have sought that Word.

Before long I found myself settled into the life of the compound. Language study gave me no problem. I enjoyed the hours when I studied alone and I was hugely diverted by my teacher, a High School student who came each morning before going to school. He was so amusing with his pillbox hat, his Norfolk jacket over a white muslin dhoti, his bare feet thrust into huge shoes. But I wouldn't have dared to laugh at him, his dignity was so enormous. He must have been a good teacher for I was soon able to converse with the Biblewomen after morning prayers and so lost my sense of isolation.

The current trouble having blown over, the girls went off to camp for the winter. Sometimes my seniors took me with them to visit the camp, to deliver mail and replenish stores. Almost before I realized it the winter was over and by the end of April I was in the hills attending the language school and reunited with my friends of the City of Paris. We sat together in class and laughed at each other's howlers. We hiked together on Saturday over the Mussourie hills, picnicking by lovely waterfalls. Then the exams behind us, I was back again in Saugor, now allowed to do more evangelistic work. And in November I joined Amy and the Bible women in camp.

If my diary tells the truth (and they don't always – not the whole truth!) that winter was the happiest period of my first term in India. We had to set up our tents in a Government camping ground. Such sites were to be found outside every large village in the sparsely populated jungle of Central India, usually in a shady mango grove and beside an excellent well. Here at regular intervals came British Government officials – forest officers, magistrates, district commissioners – to settle the affairs of the village, to listen to complaints, to solve problems and end feuds, to administer justice and collect taxes. If such a Sahib should be in residence when we arrived we would move humbly on to another mango grove, one less convenient but adequate. The officer, often profusely apologetic, would arrange for the Government watchman to see to our needs in the way of milk and eggs and firewood. Then we would see him no more.

'I never thought evangelistic work would be so interesting,' I said to my companion one evening after a long day in the villages.

I was sitting on a low stool watching the two Biblewomen cook their supper. They had coaxed a fire of dry sticks in the narrow space between two long stones. A pot of lentils bubbled at one end, sending out a most savoury smell. Mrs Wilfrid, sitting cross-legged on the grass, would give this an occasional stir as she rolled out the unleavened bread on a small board with the ingenious, circular movement that produces perfectly round, wafer thin chapattis. Mrs Sultan was baking the chapattis on a griddle, turning them deftly and then standing them on end in the hot ashes which inflated them like balloons.

Amy, two years my senior, looked up from her account book. 'Yes, it's pleasant doing it from camp when you've left all the troubles behind you in the compound. You'll learn that soon enough.'

I grinned. 'I know it now. I learned it the hard way my first week in Saugor.'

She cocked an enquiring eyebrow at me but I smiled and said nothing. The past was gone; let it go.

I looked around with contentment. The setting sun was sending long shafts of golden light between the trees and beyond the grove I could see the undulating slopes of scrubby jungle bathed in its mellow glow. To my right the smoke from dozens of small fires hovered over the village like a cloud. A few yards from where I sat stood the comfortable tent where Amy and I slept. It was a rectangular affair with double walls to protect against the sun. The cloth of the inner wall was a cheerful yellow, patterned in brown, like wallpaper. A canopy shaded the doorway and under this our small table was laid for supper. Clinging to our nice British ways we had tried to keep a vase of flowers on this table, until we heard the villagers saying, 'The foreigners' god is a pot with flowers in; they bow down to it twice a day (saying grace!) and ring a bell to wake the god (warning the cook that we were ready to eat!)'

Squatting near the tent our cook was vigorously cleaning lamp glasses, preparing for the darkness which would descend as soon as the sun dipped behind the horizon. Out of my range of vision, someone was drawing water at the well, singing a Christian hymn to the accompaniment of a squeaking pulley.

31

It was an idyllic life. Supper over, we would pray together sitting round the cook's fire where his supper would be keeping warm. Then Amy and I would retire to our tent. Tightly lacing the tent flaps against animal marauders as well as the now piercingly cold wind. We would lie listening to the murmur of voices from where the Biblewomen were making the most of the dying fire before going to their tent. Then we would fall into a deep sleep from which not even the terrifying yells of prowling jackals disturbed us.

Next morning, after breakfast and prayers, we would set out for our work, Amy and I, following the cart track on foot through the few cultivated fields around the village then out into wilder country.

The jungle of Central India is not the jungle of lush undergrowth and tropical flowers and fruits. Only in the hot season would it spring to breathtaking beauty as hundreds of Flame of Forest trees burst into bloom with salmon pink flowers on the bare branches, and the acacia thorn would put out yellow, mimosa-like blossoms. Nevertheless, even on these winter mornings Amy and I would find much to interest and delight us. We would watch the mist float away from the tops of the hills like gauzy scarves, torn by the sun and the wind. We would stop to examine a thorn bush festooned from top to bottom with spiders' webs, the dew caught on them sparkling like gems – ruby red, topaz, emerald green and amethyst. We would walk until we were tired and then join the Biblewomen in the tonga.

The tonga is a two-wheeled vehicle seating four people, two by two and back to back, not facing sideways as on the Irish jaunting car but forward and backward. Ours, made especially for travel on rough roads, was strongly built and well sprung and had a canopy to shelter us from the hot sun. It was drawn by two white trotting bullocks who were induced to trot and occasionally to gallop by our driver who sat on the dashboard and twisted their tails!

Gulab Singh was a picturesque figure. He belonged to the Kshatria or soldier caste and could have had the blood of kings running through his veins, which was perhaps why he swaggered in his walk. His black eyes sparkled above his military-style moustache which he constantly stroked with an upward movement. He wore a huge muslin turban, cleverly wound around his head to form a pleated cockade in front and a long tail behind. An old Norfolk jacket over his muslin dhoti completed his costume.

He was a good Christian. Several years earlier, walking through a field, he had picked up a page torn from a Gospel of John. Impressed by what he read he yearned to know more and went about asking people if they knew anything about it. At last a shopkeeper told him it was a Christian book and sent him to the Mission. He was given a Gospel and some tracts and some weeks later he returned a converted man, determined to become a Christian openly by taking baptism. Thrown out of his village, he became the Mission driver.

There was nothing of the servile servant about him. During our long journeys over the lonely jungle roads (often miles lay between one village and the next) he would enliven the way by singing hymns of his own composing, mostly Scripture verses set to music. Or he would carry on a lively conversation with the Biblewomen sitting behind us. He would tease gentle Mrs Sultan gallantly but hold fierce arguments with the more aggressive Mrs Wilfred.

Mrs Wilfred was of the earth, earthy! She also was one of the swaggerers. She swaggered because she had supreme confidence in herself. I have more than once heard her ask a group of village women what the two Miss Sahibs would do without her, they with their terrible Hindi, poor things! On our arrival at a village she would descend from her back seat in the tonga and sail ahead while we meekly followed. She had the strange walk that many village women have, belying the popular image most of us hold of the graceful sari clad figure carrying the water pot! With feet very much splay, stomach thrust out so that her back was not so much erect as bent backwards, sari caught between her teeth to keep it from blowing off her head, a bag of books in one hand and a huge sunshade in the other, she would enter the main village street and gather the women together with nothing more than a lordly gesture of the chin towards a shady tree. She could quell any disturbance with a look, from crying babies and cheeky youths to old crones beginning to tell a sordid story that she didn't think fit for our innocent ears. 'They don't talk about these things,' she would mutter, cocking a chin in our direction. 'They don't know anything about it, bechari (poor things!)' At this there would be exclamations of surprise and pity as the fact dawned upon them that we, big girls as we were, were not married.

But then, all curiosity satisfied, Mrs Wilfred launched into her own particular method of preaching the Gospel, she had no difficulty in keeping their attention. Her love for the Lord shone on her very homely face and there was conviction behind her words.

In these scattered villages of the great central jungle we were indeed preaching to those who had never heard the Gospel. On one occasion a man, obviously a stranger, came and stood at the back of the crowd, leaning on his staff. He listened with his mouth open and his eyes filled with wonder as Mrs Wilfred told the glories of her Lord and Saviour and in the hush that followed he said, indicating me with his chin:

'Is that he, Bua?'

At midday we would eat our lunch beside a jungle stream where nothing disturbed the stillness but the fluttering and occasional restlessness of the small birds when a kite hovered overhead. How often in later years, living among the teeming villages of N. Bihar where a private picnic spot was something only to be dreamed about, I would recall with nostalgia those quiet meals.

The afternoon meetings were easier, the people more relaxed. Household chores finished for the time being, the women would sit in groups in the mellow comforting rays of the winter sunshine. Some would have let down their hair and would be leisurely exploring each other's head, parting by parting. Some young mother, sitting on the ground, oiled the baby as it lay stretched along her legs, its head between her feet. The babies were fat and dimpled in those days, or so it seems to me looking back. The mothers oiled them, stroking the rounded limbs and the shining black heads lovingly. And they listened, some attentively and with intelligence, some indifferently, some with wistful looks as we told them about the Son of God who came to earth and died for their sins.

Now we would take the long trail home again. Sometimes we were silent, watching the shadows of the trees lengthen across the path. Sometimes Amy and I sang our English hymns, laughing triumphantly when we managed a whole hymn from memory. The two women would be holding a murmured conversation behind us and Gulab Singh thought his own long thoughts.

Too quickly that winter was over. The heat of April prohibited the living in tents and soon we were back among the burdens and heartbreaks of the Mission compound. Because of what I will be saying later, I must add here in confession that I didn't really make these heartaches my own — only when they caused my colleagues to be irritable or sad or withdrawn and so brought an uneasy, uncomfortable atmosphere into the home or compound. They were my problems only so far as they affected my happiness.

By the next winter I was transferred to Kachhwa to be an evangelist attached to the hospital there.

CHAPTER SIX

Kachhwa

It was a hostile crowd made up mainly of men and boys that filled the 'lawn' in front of our bungalow, spilling over to the doctor's house and reaching to the wall of the women's ward. The sound of their fury came through the closed windows of our sitting room. Peering through the shutters I could see their hands raised defiantly as two of our men tried to reason with them. They looked so evil, my heart pounded and I felt sick.

The cause of their anger was here with us in the room — an eighteen-year-old girl. Her eyes were frightened and at the same time defiant.

'I won't go back with them,' she was saying fiercely. 'Don't make me go with them, Miss Sahib. They don't want me at home. It's only because I want to become a Christian that they are angry.'

This was quite true. She had come to outpatients two years before, suffering from a TB elbow. Only the stench of it filling the house had forced her eldest brother, head of the house, to bring her to hospital and consent to an operation. The arm was removed from above the elbow. She was an inpatient for several weeks and then, as she lived in the village nearby, she was discharged but had to come daily for dressings.

She had formed the habit of sitting in the little school for village children held in a disused private ward and here she learned to read and write and to love the Lord Jesus Christ. She needed Him desperately, needed His love and companionship and the love of His people for she was in a miserable situation. Her parents were dead. She had been married as a child but had not yet gone to her husband. When the operation was performed, the boy's people refused to accept a one-armed bride and sought another girl. D. was as good as a widow and in those days it was better to be dead.

But D. was a naturally cheerful girl, at times an exceedingly naughty girl, full of mischief and high spirits. She loved her daily visits to the hospital, prolonging them as much as possible by deliberately choosing to be the last patient of the day, often having to be called from the school where she lorded it over the children and finally was allowed to teach the little ones. She was treated as an old friend by nurses and doctors, taught more of the Lord by evangelists, and loved by everybody. What did it matter that nobody at home wanted her, that she was a burden to her brother and a nuisance to her sisters-in law in the kitchen seeing she had only one hand?

Then the day came when her desire to be a Christian openly, to live among Christians and work in the hospital, became too strong to be resisted. She announced that she wanted to be baptized. No one knows how the news came to be known by her family but reach them it did, with the result that she was locked in a room alone. Many times in a day one brother or another went in to threaten or coerce her to give up this intention. She was cruelly beaten many times. The women pleaded with her, the men tried to bribe her but she remained adamant.

'I am a Christian' she would say. 'You can't take that away from me.'

One day she escaped and ran to us for shelter. Within hours the mob was at our doors.

We had to let her go in the end. The headman demanded her return in spite of the fact that she was of age and had stated openly her wish to live and work in the hospital. He promised that there would be no more persecution – he would see to that. So with heavy hearts and uneasy consciences we watched her go, walking with bent head behind her brother. The headman's promises were false, of course. The girl had to pass through many bitter experiences before she became a Christian openly, and finally a teacher in the little school.

This was but one of the upheavals that shook Kachhwa in those days as one and another came openly for Christ. But this one affected me most for I was newly posted there. I saw how tenacious faith can be, how much dreadful persecution the weakest believer is able to bear through Christ's upholding. But my joy was swamped by the terrifying thought that D's story was spreading over the district. I had been launched as an evangelist just when hostility was at its highest.

Hostility. This was what had made Monday afternoons at college miserable for me, breaking up the serene happiness which I couldn't do without. But there in Peckham the hostility was something imagined as I stood at some door, and which more often than not didn't materialise. But this was real.

Fortunately, I didn't have to face it every day. On alternate mornings the other evangelist, Brownie, would go off with her Biblewoman for the district, while I did duty in the outpatients department. Here I took care of the women squatting in the waiting room, entering their names in the register, handing out prescription papers and collecting their paise (the smallest coin of all). Then I would teach them to sing hymns to their own tunes, or try to, and talk to them about the Lord till the doctor arrived. When the last one had been seen by him and while he was dealing with the first batch of men, I would gather a further group of women and go through the same process.

I loved the work. There was no hostility. The women had come of their own free will; they were sick or had loved ones at home desperately ill. They needed us. They were grateful and they listened to our message whether they understood it or not.

But next morning I would have to join the Biblewoman and set off for some distant village. The more distant the village the better I was suited, not only because there would be less fear of repercussions from D's affair but because I enjoyed the journey. Just as I had enjoyed shipboard life which had delayed the moment I dreaded.

There was much to delight me during those early morning trips as we bowled along the dusty roads. The jogging bullock-tonga was a thing of the past. Here we used an ekka, a vehicle best described as a tabletop on two large, steel-rimmed wheels, on which one sat cross-legged or dangled one's legs over the side. Our ekka, hired by the month and driven by a cheerful bearded Muslim, boasted a sun canopy and was drawn by a frisky, well fed horse.

The countryside around Kachhwa was quite different from the jungle of Central India. Almost every inch of land had been put to the plough. In winter, the fields, unbroken by hedge or fence, stretched green and lovely with young wheat as far as the eye could see. In spring, the wheat was golden to harvest and the tall, misshapen shishan trees sprang into sudden beauty, the tender green of young beeches. In high summer, when the same fields were bare, grey with dust and stubble, when the heat shimmered on the road ahead of us and the hot wind from the west scorched our faces and arms, the trees were at their loveliest. We would pass a tall Indian laburnum, its cascade of yellow flowers mingling with the scarlet and orange clusters of the Gulmohar blossoms, both flung against the burning blue of a cloudless sky. When the monsoons came to devastate the towns, turning their streets into rivers of muddy water, staining the whitewashed walls of houses a dreary grey, adding dilapidation to dilapidation, ruin to ruin, the countryside would be transformed into a riot of green, the pale green of new leaves and undergrowth, the vivid emerald of paddy shoots. And every wayside pool would be like bits of fallen sky.

I would be revelling in all this when there would appear the dark red roofs of a village. 'We're here,' the Biblewoman would say and my spirits would sink to zero. I would slide reluctantly from the ekka and follow her along the path to the village. With bag of books in one hand and umbrella (for shade) in the other, my eyes sheltered by dark glasses from the curious and often lewd stares of men sitting in groups, (could any country in the world show so many men with nothing to do all day but sit), we would traverse the narrow alleys in search of women with time to sit and talk to us.

There would have been little to make me uneasy had we been left in peace with the women and the children. They loved to have us sit in their yards. We made a pleasant break in their monotonous lives, bringing news of the outside world. We gave them something to talk about, something new to see in the way of saris and materials. Our trouble began when the man of the house, perhaps warned by someone that the Christians were teaching his womenfolk, would return in a fury, angered more by the smiles of his informers than our presence in his house. Sometimes such a man would be violent, throwing our books after us and occasionally setting the dogs on us. Fortunately India's pi dogs are cowardly creatures, more yap than bite.

However, for the most part the antagonism was subtle, Indians being of all things polite, but it was equally disconcerting.

'Somebody is signalling to us from that window,' I said to the Biblewoman one day, pointing to a high window in an otherwise blank wall. We had been singing with some women under a tree and the sound must have penetrated the walls of this rich man's house.

'We'll go to the back,' said Mrs J.B. and led me to a double door in a deserted alley. This was the women's door through which they would slip out after dark or before dawn to get a breath of air and for the purpose of the toilet.

The door opened cautiously and entering we found ourselves in a large, paved courtyard. The pavement was dirty, marked with old stains and there was a strong smell of urine. There must have been thirty to forty women and girls, the latter in gaily coloured saris, some of them strikingly beautiful. One or two of these girls had babies at their breasts, and sitting at the back were the inevitable sad faced old women, widows in white saris. Someone pulled forward a stringed cot for us to sit on and they all gathered around, squatting on the ground. Naked babies crawled about our feet and the young boys stood and stared, chewing at something that takes the place of chewing gum in the villages.

'Sing!' said a woman slapping my knee. 'She knows your songs,' and she pointed to a girl of fifteen or so. The girl smiled shyly and nodded. She was the latest daughter-in-law, recently come from her home in the city where she had been taught to read by our Biblewomen.

We were enjoying a good sing, many of them humming the familiar, sad tune:

The river is wide and the boat is old,
Who will take me across but Jesus?

Suddenly a man's voice came from somewhere in front of the house, calling one of the girls. She rose and ran with a flurry of pink voile; then we heard the tinkle of cups and saucers.

'Give them a cup of tea,' he must have snarled, for in Indian villages once refreshments have been offered you are free to go, in fact you are expected to take your departure. We drank the tea and left with what dignity we could muster.

But these occasional clashes with the men folk could not wholly account for my shrinking, for my need to brace myself each time I faced a village. What else could there be that was so potent to take the joy out of my work? It wasn't the discomforts of village life – the smells, the sight of flies sitting undisturbed on a child's dirty nose, the filthy beds on which one had at times to sit, the fear of germs. None of these things moved me. I once drank without blanching a cup of warm milk, sugared and stirred with a doubtful forefinger. I drank it because I had refused a cup of un-boiled water, distressing a woman who was following her village code that for the poor, a cup of cold water offered freely fulfilled the law of hospitality. Once, sitting on a filthy cot, I didn't turn a hair when a woman emerged from an inner room, black with smallpox. And during epidemics of plague which visited us often in those days when whole villages were deserted, left to the plague-filled rats, while the inhabitants camped on the open plains, even then I shrank more from the injections we were given and which had the most painful reactions than I did from continuing my work in the district.

In fact, I was quite at home in village company provided it was friendly, whether sitting outside the huts of the very poor or in the sheltered courtyard of the ordinary farming folk. These yards, open to the sky and formed by four low roofed rooms would be sharply divided, half in bright sunshine and half in shade, shade as cool as a cup of water. Since the sunlight was not glittering on white walls but on the khaki of cow dung plaster it was mellow and easy on the eyes. The place would be uncluttered, the only furniture a stringed cot on which grain would be drying and a heap of aluminium pots winking in the sun by the low fireplace. Sitting with my back to the wall in such a courtyard I would feel the spell of village life steal over me in a most extraordinary way.

One day, seated in such a yard, my eyes fixed dreamily on the yellow flowers of a pumpkin vine which sprawled over the roof in front of me, everything seemed to me so peaceful, so right. Then I became aware of the group of women squatting on the ground by Mrs J.B. Tears were trickling down the cheeks of the one who was talking and there was a look of such stony despair on her face that I was startled out of my complacency. I could almost hear the tinkle as the illusion of peace was shattered.

'What was that woman saying to you?' I asked Mrs J. B. on the way home. 'The one who was crying.'

'Her little daughter has been widowed. She was only married a few months ago. When the news came, her brothers went to bring her home but they refused to let her come — even for a visit.'

'But why? How could they prevent her coming home? I know that a wife is completely in the power of her mother-in-law but what right has she to keep the girl when the husband is dead?'

'It is the custom. She belongs to the susarel — the house of her in-laws.'

'Oh,' I said. 'Now I see why the women in outpatients looked so sceptical when I told them what we say in the West — A son's a son till he takes a wife, a daughter's a daughter all her life! — It's absolutely the opposite here. Oh, the poor girls! No wonder they wail when they are being taken to their husbands. I've seen them staggering along the road to the station, a few yards behind the brother who is escorting them. How old is this girl?'

'Thirteen.'

I was shocked into silence. All the joy had gone out of the day for me. I tried to turn my thoughts to pleasanter things but Mrs J. B. dragged them back.

'You are going to lose Gulabi from the school this week.' She said. 'She is going to her husband.'

Gulabi was about twelve years old and one of our brightest girls. She was desperately poor, a child of the Outcaste community. (We called them Outcaste or Untouchables in those days. Many years were to pass before Mr Gandhi forbade the title and called them *Harijans* — Children of God.)

'But I didn't know she was married.' I cried.

'She isn't. She will be married when she gets there – in a fashion. The poorer Outcastes don't go in for grand weddings. Some of them don't bother with a ceremony at all. They just give their daughters to any man prepared to have them. They have given Gulabi to an old man.' Seeing my stricken look she said flatly, 'There was no dowry. And Gulabi is *ek dum kala* — quite black. There were no other offers.'

And I had been thinking there was something good about village life — so uncluttered, so quiet. I had mistaken the placidity on the faces of the poorer village women for peace when it was simply patient endurance of age-old sorrows, acceptance when there is no other way but to endure.

Someone will say: 'But is it not true that in acceptance lies peace?'

Of course it is true. The lives of these village women would be intolerable if they were to begin to fight against the injustice of their lot. Their acceptance does bring a measure of peace but how can it be true peace of heart? That can only come to those who know that the grief, the pain, the crushing blow has been allowed by a loving God who cares, a God who has power to bring good out of evil, a God who loved so much that He came among us and walked the same way of sorrow. In this sort of acceptance there is more than peace — there can be deep joy.

But who was I, young and light-hearted, dodging trouble whenever I saw it coming, knowing nothing of real affliction — who was I, I say, to talk to such women of joy in sorrow?

Mrs J. B.'s account of the two desolate little girls may not sound so horrifying to modern ears as they did to mine. Sorrow and suffering seem to have increased since those quiet years before the war. Or is it that the media has brought the world's pain into our very homes? We hear so much that we are becoming used to it. We feel a momentary pang of pity as we hear of the physical suffering of millions, the hunger and the homelessness, but these sufferings we can do a little to alleviate by putting our hands in our pockets. Thus we can ease the burden of a slightly guilty conscience. We have perhaps forgotten the stories of the suffering of mind and spirit we used to hear about in missionary meetings, the agonies of child widows and childless wives, the helplessness of the poor against powerful and unscrupulous men who remove ancient landmarks and rob widows and orphans; the helplessness of an ignorant people against cruel gods of a superstitious religion who demand outrageous sacrifices and give nothing in return. We may even have begun to suspect that the stories were fabrications to be used as propaganda. But they were not.

Or perhaps we expostulate and say that these sorrows of the mind and spirit are not unknown to us here, that they are all about us. But, writing as I am now from Ulster where horror strikes daily in our streets, I know where the difference lies between our afflictions and those of my now far-away villagers. Here there is neighbourly sympathy and helpfulness to ameliorate the agony of loss and bereavement but there I sensed a dreadful loneliness about much of their suffering. I could see no sign of sympathy on the impassive faces of neighbours as they listened to some tale of woe. Nobody seemed to care.

This is, of course, inevitable in a community where people really believe that calamity and disaster are evidence of the disapproval of greatly feared gods. Onlookers, even friends and relations tend to stand aloof, fearful least that disapproval cast its shadow over them. This aloofness can become sheer cruelty as in the case of an outbreak of smallpox, for instance. To the villagers, this was a sign that the goddess Kali, the Black One, had passed that way and laid her hand on one and another. Therefore no medicine must be given for that disease. Nor for anything else until the spots had been dry for ten days. More than once in later years I have stood helplessly by while a neighbour or one of my village Sunday School children died, not from the smallpox itself but from some complication — dysentery or bronchitis which we were not allowed to treat. And we all know what happens to those found suffering from leprosy.

In the cities and among the educated where the iron bands of custom and caste are loosening and where superstition is losing its grip, the cruel treatment meted out to widows may be softening but in the villages a widow is still considered the cause of her husband's death and so an object of the wrath of the gods. She is but working out the expiation of some sin committed in a past existence. There is no sympathy for her as she is stripped of her jewels and bright garments and condemned to the life of an unprotected woman in a house full of unrelated men. Only her mother grieves in a faraway village.

One hopes that the mental agony of the childless wife may also be lessening in some sections of society. But to the man who really believes that a son is necessary to light his funeral pyre and ensure his safe passage from this life to the next, a childless wife is more than a disappointment — she is a curse.

'That is why you find village work so hard,' said my colleague Brownie after I had told her of the two little girls. It was Saturday afternoon and she was squatting on the bedroom floor cooking fudge over a Primus stove. 'You come face to face, day after day, with suffering, the sort you would never hear of if you were teaching in a school or working in the wards.'

'They see enough suffering in the wards, surely,' I said.

She didn't answer at once. She was testing the syrup in a cup of cold water. It wasn't ready so she resumed her stirring and turned to me. 'I don't mean physical suffering;' she said. 'I mean the mental suffering. It comes during that half hour when Mrs J. B. is listening to the women before we ask them to listen to us; it wrings your heart but you are helpless to do anything.'

That could be it. I was young enough to resent having my heart constantly wrung by other people's troubles.

There was a rich man's demesne near our home in a huge place surrounded by a high wall. The man was something in the city. We would see him occasionally going off to his work in an opulent car and dressed in immaculate western garb. Sometimes Mrs J.B. and I would visit his three wives. He was a Hindu and as such was forbidden to have more than one wife but the rich had a way of avoiding the law. We would spend as little time as politeness allowed with the current wife who was fat, lazy and arrogant. Sitting in the main courtyard, a spacious place where doves cooed and fluttered, where water tinkled from a fountain in the centre and flowering shrubs scented the air, she would treat us with scarcely veiled contempt, languidly waving us on when we asked permission to visit the other ladies.

Passing through two small rooms, all stone paved and scrupulously clean, we would enter the quarters of the two discarded wives, and would settle down for an hour or more of intimate discussion. The ladies were middle aged and already white-haired. They wore no jewellery and were dressed in plain white saris as if they were already widowed. Their quarters were clean and bare and for years they had never once stepped outside the threshold of that small courtyard. They saw nobody save the old woman who came to sweep the floors and clean out the commodes, and occasionally the arrogant young wife.

They were pathetically grateful for our visits and for the opportunity to converse with intelligent people, for they themselves were intelligent, cultured women, able to read Sanskrit and fully versed in their own scriptures, the Vedas. They spoke the Hindi I had learned at language school so I was able to converse with them freely, to appeal to them in a way I could not with the villagers. They had copies of our Bible and there was always a great wistfulness about them as they discussed the meaning of the Gospel. The degrading, humiliating treatment they had suffered had gone deep and the beautiful, comforting words of the Gospel appealed to them as did the compassion of the Lord Jesus Christ, His tenderness toward women and His final sacrificing of Himself for others.

But the truth never, as far as I know, broke through the barrier of their terrible fear of the next life or from their own way of preparing to face it. The belief was firmly fixed that only by daily offerings before the sacred tulsi plant that grew from a pillar in the centre of the yard, by constant, unwearyingly chanting of prayers and by meditation on the Vedas could they hope to expiate the sin of a past existence for which they were now suffering and merit for themselves a better chance in the next, the bliss, perhaps of being born a man.

They clung to this hope and dared not leave it, dared not take the risk of trusting expiation for sin that someone else had suffered in love for them and bought for them at the cost of His blood. Their thirst remained un-slaked by the Water of Life which can spring up in the heart to everlasting life, because they dare not stop to drink.

I knew that in myself I could do nothing for any of these women, rich or poor. But surely, I thought, Jesus could. I had never known such deep sorrow, such inescapable anguish but I had known His power to comfort and strengthen in smaller trials. If only these women would touch Him! It wouldn't matter to Him whether they were poor and ignorant or intelligent and learned. If they would only open their hearts to Him they would find, as the woman at the well of Samaria found, that He does not have to draw His life-giving gift from their own well, from the depths of their stunted personalities or from the depths of their sorrows. Not even from the shallows of my poor experiences. His gifts are from above, who said: "The water that I shall give him will become in him a spring of water welling up to eternal life."

The most distressing experience of all for us was to see someone coming to the brink of drinking and turning away.

'Where is Jasoda?' I asked one day as we entered a familiar village and no Jasoda had come running to meet us. She had sat at our feet always and listened with joy. She too was a widow — a young widow, and the story of God's love had always moved her intensely.

41

A woman pointed with her chin toward the well. Jasoda was sitting there with her back to us. I left Mrs J. B. to carry on and going over to the well sat down beside Jasoda on the ground. For some time she remained stubbornly silent to my questions but at last she spoke.

'Why ever did you come? I was happy before you came but now I can never be happy again.'

Shocked and disturbed by her outburst, I tried to show her that she was unhappy because she was rejecting what she knew to be the truth. Could she not trust the Lord, take Him into her heart and life and see what He could do for her and through her?

She swept an arm in a circle, taking in the whole village. 'If what your Bible says is true, then all these are lost. I've decided that I'd rather go to hell with my friends and relatives than to heaven with strangers and foreigners!'

But in her bitterness, born, I believe, of her helplessness, Jasoda was forgetting one thing and ignoring another. She was forgetting that she had not been happy before we came; she had been a miserable, lonely woman into whose life we had brought some interest and hope. And she was ignoring the fact that, according to the faith to which she was turning back, she would go neither to heaven or hell with her friends and relatives; she would go out alone — alone and uncomforted into some unknown, unspeakably horrible place where her spirit would roam for a short time and then return, into what form she knew not. Maybe not even a human form, but a dog to be kicked around or an insect to be squashed underfoot. She would never again see or know any of her friends. She would simply be somebody or something else.

We had offered her a Saviour who would never forsake her. Who would be with her all through her troubled life and hold her hand as she crossed the dark river. He would lead her Home, to the Father's house where there will be no more sorrow or crying, no more loneliness and bitterness of spirit because there will be no sin, no cruelty and oppression, no greed, no selfishness.

Jasoda was the only person I met during my long years in the country to put into stark words the question that must haunt every evangelist at times. Would it have been better for these people had they never heard? Were we exposing them to a judgement they might otherwise have escaped? There is no doubt that those who have heard and recognised the truth of the Gospel but then reject it often become its greatest opponents and in themselves become hard and bitter. The Apostle Paul says that our knowledge of God which we are spreading throughout the world is as a lovely perfume to Him and also to all those who by grace through faith are being saved. But to those who do not believe, who are heading for death, it has the smell of doom. And, he adds: 'Who could think himself adequate for such a responsibility?' (2 Cor. 2: 15, 16 - Phillips)

The Biblewomen and I didn't try to reason all this out. Driving home, we were silent — because of what had happened but trying to comfort ourselves with the thought that God knows what is in the heart, whatever the lips may say. We could safely leave Jasoda in His hands for 'Shall not the Judge of all the earth do right?'

CHAPTER SEVEN

Inner Conflict

Perhaps it was this sad encounter with Jasoda, coming towards the end of my seventh year in India, that added a sense of frustration to my shrinking. I began to question the efficiency, even the wisdom of our method of evangelism. How could we convince the villagers that Christ belonged to India as well as to Britain when all the evangelism was being done by foreigners? To Jasoda, even the national Christians were strangers and aliens.

'That's because most Christians are huddled in or around Christian compounds,' said Brownie to whom I had revealed my frustration. 'We are all lumped together in their minds as part of the British Government. But after all, many of these converts who are with us are here because they have been thrown out of home and village. The villagers can't have it every way. We don't want converts to settle in the compound but we can't turn them adrift. Nor do we like women converts running away to us. It doesn't help our work when the villagers get it into their heads that every wretchedly unhappy girl who runs away is hiding in the Mission, when probably she has thrown herself down a well or under a train!'

'But at least, the few who try to run away to us have accepted our message, have understood it. For the most part you and I are spending our lives talking to women who have never been taught to think. It must take all the intelligence these poorer village women possess to grasp even the gist of what we are saying, let alone the implications of our message, that it concerns them personally and that they must do something about it. And how can they retain what they have grasped when they see us only once in a blue moon, some of them never again?'

Brownie had no answer to this and my thoughts were desperate. If only we had some Christian families in the villages, not paid preachers set up as out-station workers but indigenous families, earning their own living and witnessing to Christ by their lives and their words. If only there had been a Christian family in Jasoda's village or in a neighbouring village, to whom she could have gone for help or for a little teaching, however simple. Or most of all, for fellowship with like-minded people. But in the whole wide expanse of our district there was not one Christian family outside the Christian compound.

No indication of coming change in the pattern of service came to give us hope, but in a few years the 2nd World War along with Independence would alter the face of India and to some extent our methods of spreading the Gospel. Depleted missionary personnel in the country would cause full-time foreign evangelists to become almost extinct. Growing literacy would put a new importance on evangelism through literature; the owning of a transistor set would become a status symbol and radio evangelism would beam the message to the most remote villages. Biggest change of all would be among Christians. A new spirit of independence would send them out into a wider field of work, many into civil service which would scatter them abroad to fulfil, where there was love for the Lord and integrity of character, my present longing. But the day was yet a long way off when nationals would lead the way in the field of evangelism, in the 1930s it was just a dream. For us there was only the slow, steady infiltration into our vast, thickly populated areas, moving from village to village, with no real hope of touching every place even once.

All the same, it was futile, even sinful of me to allow myself to become frustrated by lack of results. These methods were undoubtedly bringing success in some parts of India, but we were working in the Ganges valley, the bedrock of Hinduism and the Lord Himself acknowledged that the results of the sowing of the seed of the Word would depend to a great extent on the soil into which it falls. It was not our responsibility to produce fruit; that was the work of the Spirit. He had been sent and neither of us doubted that we had been sent to be witnesses to Christ, to make His name known in one of the uttermost parts of the world. We were working alongside busy doctors and nurses so that together we might accomplish what the Lord had told us to do, to teach, to preach and to heal. We were sowing the seed of the Lord in season and out of season. We preached the Gospel, we talked the Gospel and we sang the Gospel, teaching the songs in the way illiterate people have been taught from the beginning of time. Using their own tunes we sang each line twice, encouraging the women to sing the repeat after us.

I ought to have left all this with the Lord. I ought to have been content to be a sower, leaving the results to God who alone gives the increase. But I was in a state of restlessness. I had also been feeling unwell for some time. I have memories of hot-season mornings when, wakened at dawn by the sound of my colleagues rising from their beds (we slept in a line on the veranda), I would stagger into the house, the heat and stale air meeting me like the smack of a hot, unsavoury hand. In my room I would sink into the low chair where I usually sat for my quiet time and would remain there, exhausted, doing nothing until it was time to dress for prayers in church. Then after breakfast there would be the usual bracing of myself to face another village.

There was nothing seriously wrong — just a sort of malaise that I could throw off when in company of others but which descended upon me like a cloud when I was alone, sapping my energy.

But the discouragements of my work were not the only cause of my sickness. Through them all I had been buoyed up by my natural optimism. It wouldn't always be like this, I thought. I wouldn't have to go on doing this hard, unrewarding work all my life. There would be a change sometime. In fact, I was sure a change was coming; I had seen it in my day-dreams. Day-dreaming being an art at which I was an adept, I could always find a way of escape from my troubling thoughts by this delightful pastime. So low must I have shrunk spiritually at this time that I could day-dream in the village square while Mrs J.B. talked to the women. Sheltered behind my dark-glasses I could close my eyes and float away into a world of my own where I was the centre of everything and everything was working out my way.

How dangerous is this form of escapism. How it unfits one to face reality, to meet the sudden devastating disappointments of life; the reality which one day I found myself unable to face the probability that some of my rosy dreams of the future were not coming true. There was going to be no change in my circumstances. Suddenly the prospect loomed before me of years filled with that which cost me so much — the frustrating, exhausting, discouraging task of preaching, every day, week in week out, year in and year out, to unresponsive villagers. Nothing exciting was going to happen to me. Nothing was going to change.

Then I knew a period of rebellion against God and His will for my life. This had never happened before. I had been dismayed by His revealed will, had been reluctant to follow it, but I had accepted it, even desired it. But now I was fighting. My dreams had built for me a picture of a future that I felt was right for me. It was the only way to happiness and fulfilment for me. When I began to suspect that it was not God's way for me, I rebelled.

My prayers now matched my dreams. I was the centre of them, filling them to the exclusion of everybody and everything else. I prayed with supplication. I reminded the Lord of every verse I knew which promised that fervent and believing-prayer was always answered. I battered at heaven's gate determined to make the Lord see that what I wanted was the right thing for me.

Then one Sunday I was suddenly tired of it all. I longed to cease from battering and from wrestling with God, to know again the rest and peace of acceptance. But I found that the desire my dreams had fashioned refused to be gone. It had me in chains. In vain I offered it up to the Lord, pleading with Him to remove this root cause of my unrest, my wrong thoughts; my unfruitful service. It refused to stay on the altar. It took a miracle of God to set me free and it happened at a day of prayer gathering.

The day of prayer had been enjoyable, a most interesting and thought-provoking time. The speaker for this special occasion, a middle aged man, would today be called a Christian psychologist. He was said to have psychic powers including water-divining and he had taken us into the problems of the subconscious. He insisted among other things that every traumatic experience we had known – every deep hurt, every bout of rage, every surge of hate — that had not be placed under the cleansing blood of Christ was still working its ill in our subconscious. He said that it was the Blood of Christ, not our repenting, not our forgiving or our trying to forget, that deals with and cleanses away the effect of past resentments and hurts.

His fresh approach to the subject of cleansing and forgiveness had claimed our attention through two long meetings. One had to muster all one's powers of concentration in order to follow him and keep hold of the thread. We had forgotten how cold we were on this January day, how bitter the draughts that seeped under the four doors of the Mirzapur sitting-room, how our feet were freezing on the stone floor. But now, meetings over, we were enjoying fellowship over a cup of tea before taking our different ways. The tables had been set in the garden and we were grateful for the warmth of the late afternoon sunshine.

The speaker sat opposite me at the table and several times I saw his eyes rest speculatively on me. So I was not surprised and a little flattered, when he said to me as we rose from the table: 'Will you show me round the garden?'

He didn't need to be shown around. Everything there in the garden was in full view, the glowing poinsettia bushes that had reached the proportion of trees, the delicate scarlet hibiscus, the pink oleander blooms in their nests of glossy leaves. He was as familiar as I with an Indian garden; probably had the same purple bougainvillea climbing over the screen of his own verandah. But I went.

'Now, what is the trouble?' he asked when we were out of earshot. 'What are you fighting against?'

I looked up at him in surprise. I had been my brightest self all day and with a brightness that was not assumed. It was my usual reaction when in company of a crowd of people. All my troubles were temporarily forgotten. I shook my head and said: 'Nothing!'

He smiled. 'Now, don't make wide eyes at me. I know you are full of inner conflict. It would help if you could tell me.'

I cannot remember what I told him — probably something of the problems of my work. I certainly didn't divulge my secret problem. And there was not much time for deep conversation; my party from Kechchwa were ready to go and waiting for me.

'Will you promise me one thing?' the preacher said 'Will you pray this prayer every day?' "No part dark, Lord. Let there be no part dark, especially in my thinking." 'Will you?'

I promised, and ran to join the rest. Being an honest person I began at once that very night to pray the prayer. And I prayed it thoughtfully and sincerely, and next morning the Lord began to answer it though I didn't see it as an answer at the time. We had started the long trip to some distant village, Mrs J.B. and I. She was in a quiet mood and I was left with my thoughts. They ran something like this:

Conflict: The preacher said I was full of conflict. Am I? I don't know. I'm not happy. I'm restless and depressed. I'm a rotten missionary; nobody knows how useless I am. And, deep down, I'm lonely — not because I don't get on with the others; I do. They're dears. But I don't really matter to anyone. I don't come first with anyone. I suppose most Miss Sahibs feel like this at some time. We're half a world away from those who really belong to us, those who really care. Things go wrong; one's heart is in turmoil of misery and there is no shoulder to weep on.

What else? Now I'm in bondage to something that won't let me go. It's ruining my quiet times; spoiling my work. I'm frightened because God isn't answering my prayers. He will neither give me what I want — and He could — nor will He set me free. I'm frightened when I think of the future. I think God is going to leave me here, doing the same hard, unfulfilling work all my life. Until I'm on old woman. And I'm not willing. I'm fighting.

Conflict: I'm fighting against my circumstances, against my dreary future. That means I'm fighting against God. I never meant it to be this way. That Saturday evening in Preston how long ago it seems, when I realized that Jesus was actually living in me, I saw all that He could do in me and through me if only He had my whole heart. I gave myself to Him. That meant that I was asking Him to take over my life, to order my circumstances as He thought best for me. It meant His choosing my future. I was hilariously willing then — but I'm not willing now. I can't be willing. If I were, I wouldn't be fighting. Oh, Lord Jesus I'm so tired of fighting, If only I could be free from this thing which is too strong for me. I'll have no peace until it is gone.

Suddenly I seemed to hear a voice. It was so clear that I thought for a moment it was Mrs J.B. speaking. I looked at her but she was lost in thought, gazing over the vast expanse of wheat glittering like silver in the morning sunshine.

You don't really want to give it up do you?

I stared at the thought, aghast. Could it be true? Had I been deluding myself into thinking I wanted to be free? Had I been clinging to the emotion because it added some excitement to my life — gave me something to dream about when I was bored? It can't be true. I've wept as I pleaded to be delivered.

But it is true. Without this hope, this dream, life would be even more colourless and meaningless. Unless God works a miracle and gives me something in its place – the joy of His presence again; the joy of conscious fellowship with Him; the thrill of exploring the Bible and finding it living and meaningful. All that I have lost.

'We're here,' said Mrs J.B.

I slid from the ekka and picking up my bag of books I followed her along the narrow path to the village, the dew drenched vines of the field-peas wetting her sari and the hem of my frock.

That same afternoon, my work over, I went up to the flat roof of our bungalow in search of solitude — with warmth. Even at four o'clock the winter sunshine was comforting while inside the house the cold was intense. Our fire would not be lit for some time yet; the medicals didn't finish work until around six and it was assumed that no one would need a fire before then.

I sat on the parapet, the stones warm beneath me, and the whole compound was within my view. To the right was the high wall of the Nurses' Home and in front of me the circular lawn — if one can call a patch of dried-up grass by such a name! — with its borders of flowering shrubs, oleander, hibiscus and the sweet smelling jasmine. The little Christian cemetery lay beyond this with the doctors' house on the right. To my left rose the walls of the female ward and beyond it the two-storied male ward, the two buildings joined by the operating room. A large pond divided these buildings from the outpatient department and dispensary which were behind me, and across the pond I could see the homes of the Christians.

I heard a commotion below me, some laughter and the shuffling of sandals in the dust. A group of girl nurses came into view, their starched white caps looking slightly ridiculous from this vantage point, their figures foreshortened, their arms against the white aprons a varied brown from burnt umber to chocolate. They were student nurses coming from a lecture in Dorothy's or Kay's room. At the corner they parted, some going to the ward the rest passing beneath me to their quarters. Bathsheba, looking up and seeing me, waved.

'Come for a walk with us,' she called.

I shook my head. 'Not today. Tomorrow, perhaps.'

'Tomorrow never comes,' she called back with a cheeky grin.

At the door of their home, they knocked, rattling the chain against the wood. The door opened and they disappeared. Over to the left I could see Miriam coming swiftly toward the house, the wings of her cap waving rhythmically with every stride. One of the doctors emerged from his house and crossed our lawn on his way to the wards; then there was silence. Or so I wrote in my diary afterwards, but there must have been the usual sounds around me, the cawing of crows coming home to roost, the squealing of a pulley rope at the well, the sound from the road behind me of someone clearing his throat and spitting, the rattle of aluminium saucepans from the kitchen where the cook was preparing our supper. We called the meal 'dinner' in those days, however frugal it might be, but this evening, judging by the lovely aroma wafting in my direction, we were to eat curry. It would be curried meat - goat meat - eaten with delicious purees. These are unleavened bread, rolled out flat like chapattis but fried in hot fat instead of being baked dry on a griddle.

The wooden bolt in the door of the nurses' house squealed. The girls were coming out for their walk. I turned my back to the road and shut my eyes. I wanted to be alone to think out my problem. Inner conflict, the preacher had called it. It was now looming before me, not as something to be sorry for myself about, but as something sinful: something cutting me off from fellowship with God.

I hadn't thought of myself as being shut off from God, not until now. For weeks I had been praying oftener and more fervently than ever before in my life. I'd wept as I prayed. I'd wrestled with God in prayer. Why, I thought, does all this suddenly seem wrong? Are we not meant to wrestle with God? Jacob did. But God had to hurt him before he let go and allowed himself to be blessed. God is hurting me now. He is not answering my prayers.

I sighed and opened my Bible at Psalm 37. It opened of itself at the place, for I had been turning to it every day for weeks, for comfort. Did it not promise, over and over, that God would give me the desires of my heart provided they were not evil? I began to read but today the message appeared new and unfamiliar. The conditions God was setting out for answered prayers were different from what I had been reckoning on. There they were, one after the other:

"Fret not. Trust in the Lord. Delight thyself in the Lord. Rest in the Lord.
Wait patiently for Him. Commit thy way to Him."

It was the very opposite of struggling and striving. It meant trusting. Resting and waiting.
I turned to Matthew 6. "Take no thought for the morrow... Your heavenly Father knows that you have need of these things." Your heavenly Father. Had I forgotten that God is my Father, loving me, caring for me, wanting the best for me?

"He knows, He loves, He cares. Nothing this truth can dim.
He gives the very best to those who leave the choice with Him."

I've quoted these words often enough. I've written them in autograph albums. But now it isn't just a lovely, comforting verse; it's a challenge. It's frightening. Do I believe it? Do I believe that I can trust God with my future? I have to decide. I want to believe it. I believed it that Saturday night when I gave myself wholly to Him. I sang as I walked home; "I'll go where you want me to go, dear Lord.... I'll be what you want me to be." But then I was walking on air. I thought everything was going to be marvellous from then on. The Lord would make me the sweet and gentle person I longed to be and all would be sunshine.

But now I'm facing a future that looks bleak and lonely and hard. Do I believe it now? Do I believe that whatever happens to me it will be right because it will be His choice? Whether I like it or not? Whether it is my way or entirely opposed to my way? Can I trust the Lord like that? Now?

Lord, I believe. Help my unbelief. My one desire is to do Your will and be at peace. I will trust you.

The sun had gone and it had become chilly on the roof. I rose and walked to the steps, conscious of no exhilaration, not even a sense of release. But I was free. That which had tormented me for weeks had gone. The following days were to prove how completely God had freed me.
Freed from the self-centred praying, the frantic searching for comforting texts, I found my quiet times with God revolutionised. The Word was again living and powerful. It revealed for one thing why after years of Christian experience I could still have such inner conflict. I saw that, years ago, when the Holy Spirit had come into my life at my invitation, to make me what God would have me be, to use me when and how and where He should choose. He had immediately taken up issue with my old nature as Paul said He would. "Your lower nature... sets itself against the Spirit while the Spirit fights against it. They are in conflict with one another." (Gal.5.17) The Holy Spirit was fighting my old nature for me. And the conflict had been prolonged distressingly because I had fought on the wrong side — fought against Him, not liking His methods. Not when they hurt.
Now I saw that the Holy Spirit had simply been bringing me into situations where all my vows were to be tested, where my declared love for Him, my loyalty, my vaunted obedience – in fact,

everything I had believed in my heart or knew in my head — could become part of my experience, tested and found durable.

Why had I not seen this before?

I didn't need to ask anybody; I knew. I hadn't wanted to see. I had steadfastly refused to consider the place of suffering in the purposes of God. All my efforts had been concentrated on evading trouble and distress, clutching at my personal happiness which I had considered to be my right. When it was threatened, I blamed my circumstances and fought against them. When they hemmed me in so that I couldn't escape, I had fretted until I had brought myself to the verge of a nervous breakdown, a missionary casualty, beaten by circumstances.

There is a significance we often miss in the pronouns used by Paul in 1 Corinthians 3:9. Speaking of himself and Apollus, he said to the Corinthian Christians: "Ye are workers together with God. Ye are God's husbandry." Husbandry? Field. The Corinthian Christians were fields - God's fields, of course, but simply fields. Something to be dug up and turned over, to be raked, cleared of stones and rubbish, to be harrowed and ploughed, softened and made ready for the seed that would bring forth fruit. They were not yet fellow-workers with Lord on other men's fields.

Looking back to this time of my upheaval, I have to confess that I was not yet a labourer with God. I still needed much harrowing and ploughing to bring me to maturity. I hadn't wanted to be a fellow-labourer with God when it meant sharing His sorrows. I'd been a missionary for seven years and I was still a field.

C.S. Lewis puts it more clearly than I can. "God had not been trying an experiment on my faith or love in order to find out their quality, He knew it already. It was I who didn't. In this trial He makes us occupy the dock, the witness box and the bench all at once. He always knew that my temple was a house of cards. His only way of making me realize it was to knock it down."

But an infinitely kind Heavenly Father is He who wounds and binds up again. In the days that followed, during a short spell in bed while I got rid of a cold, He gave me some comforting thoughts. The Lord Jesus Christ knew what it was to shrink from a coming ordeal. Not that there is any comparison between that which He faced and the things from which I shrink. But He knew all about the shrinking of the flesh; He had sweat drops of blood as He prayed: "If it be possible, let this cup pass from Me."

This meant that there is nothing sinful about shrinking, nothing to be ashamed of. An over-vivid imagination can be the cause. It is not what we feel that matters but what we do, I remembered the story the Lord told of the young man who, when told by his Father to go and work in the vineyard said: "No. I don't want to go!" but later he repented and went. The Lord justified him rather than his brother who had said blithely: "Yes, I'll go!" but didn't go at all.

I knew now that it was better to have felt the reluctance and yet obeyed, than to have talked about the will of God, talked about the call, and not responded.

My daily work now took on a different aspect. I still had to brace myself to face a possibly antagonistic village but I was not now drawing strength to face it from the depths of early morning exhaustion. I was better in health than I had been for some time.

I found a new fellowship with Mrs J.B. as we bowled along the dusty roads and enjoyed the fresh morning air together. February is perhaps the loveliest time of the year in North India and now the countryside had even more charm for me — the vast expanse of young, green wheat, the blue sky beginning to take on the deeper sapphire of summer, the dewdrops sparkling like gems on the cobwebs festooning the thorn bushes; the exquisite turquoise of a jay's wing as it flashed across the road.

'That's good luck for today!' the Muslim driver would mutter, turning to watch the bird's flight. But we would smile at each other. What did we care for luck?

I still sheltered behind my dark glasses as we walked past the groups of idle men, still felt the old clutch at my stomach at the first sign of hostility. But the work was now full of interest. Whether Mrs J.B. talked or I, my heart was in it.

I never wrote to the preacher to thank him for the help he had given me. In fact, it was some time before I connected him and his suggested prayer with my release. Then I met him later when he paid a short visit to Dr Everard and I was able to tell him how grateful I was, he told me in front of the others that I had a good 'aura' — that there were great things ahead of me; which was a little embarrassing. There were great things ahead of us all, great opportunities if only we were ready to grasp them. Above all, there were great changes ahead of us all. In a few months the 2nd World War would burst upon the world, changing, as I said, the face of India and in many ways the pattern of missionary work.

In the meantime I had experienced changes in my own circumstances. I had been transferred to our work in the city to relieve two colleagues for furlough. I was to supervise the work of four Biblewomen as well as a thriving Babyfold. Accompanying one or another of these women I found visiting so much easier. We were visiting homes to which we had been invited to teach some shut-in girl or women to read. Although we used the Bible as a text book, no one objected. We had something to give them and so we were welcome.

Three of us were living together, Edith, my friend of the City of Paris, Connie newly out from home and busy with language study, and myself. Connie and I had some hilarious fun together while Edith smiled upon us indulgently. Then Edith was stricken with sciatica and had to go home, leaving me in charge of a large girls' school. The school had an excellent headmistress and presented no problems but the hostel bristled with them. Ethel had been sent to help us but she too was a village evangelist and had had no experience in institutional work and certainly not in dealing with excessively difficult schoolgirls. My most vivid memory of those months is of Ethel's eyebrows suddenly shooting up to the hairline and a look of consternation spreading over her very expressive face as she spotted old Buaji, the hostel's fat and amiable matron, waddling up our drive, bringing another problem.

It would happen, evening after evening, and I would have to get up and face some stubborn, unco-operative, sulky schoolgirl. Sometimes a whole dormitory full. As I worked among these girls I was saddened by every evidence of their rebellious, often unclean hearts and minds. They were the future Christian wives and mothers. The well-being of the church in our area depended upon them to a great extent and the present state of the church was disturbing enough. We longed to see these girls grow into clean, upright, gracious Christian women, born again of the Spirit. Sometimes they were responsive; we would see a marked change in the behaviour of one or two who had been difficult. Then something would happen, something shameful, and we would be sent to our knees by our apprehension that we might not be able to cope with the situation. The change in my circumstances had not brought an end to my problems. They simply changed their character.

Someone has said, and how true it proves to be, that we have to die on one level in order to operate on another. Each painful crisis, when something of ourselves dies, can lift us a little higher on to another plane where we find, not that all our problems are solved but that we face a different sort of temptation, a fresh set of problems. This I can say — I was no longer simply a field. The problems that now sent me to my knees were no longer simply my own selfish affairs; they were the Lord's problems, the problems of the care of the Church. He was allowing me to share His sorrows. I was becoming a worker together with Him

CHAPTER EIGHT

Unexpected Changes

But a greater change was coming my way. That summer, the summer of 1938, found me unexpectedly enjoying a holiday in Landour.

I say unexpectedly because, six years before, my final examinations behind me, I had said goodbye to Landour and the Language School, determined never to return, as were others of my fellow students. It was not that we disliked the place. We had found much to please and to thrill us in this small hill resort in the foothills of the Himalayas, but we had perforce spent two summers there, studying to make ourselves proficient enough in Hindi or Urdu to be able to communicate easily with the people we had come to serve. And as the principal of the school had said more than once when referring to our preaching of the Gospel or our teaching: 'You cannot say you have communicated until your hearers have fully understood what you have been saying.'

So we had studied hard knowing that ahead of us were exams, exams of a high standard (matriculation level) set by the North India Language Examination Board for people committed to a lifetime in India and which must be passed if we were not to be sent home!

This hurdle behind us, we were free to take our summer break in any one of the lovely hill resorts India offers, all of which were available to us and within our means. In the north there was Srinagar in the beautiful Vale of Kashmir. Here we could relax and recuperate on a hired houseboat moored in some quiet waterway where brilliantly coloured bulbuls dart among the reeds and the irises line the banks. Or we could drift across the lotus-starred Dal Lake in a shikara (a gondola-like craft attached to every houseboat) to picnic in the Shalimar Gardens. Or we could visit the shops along the banks of the River Jhelum which flows through the city, seeking presents for faraway friends from among the wealth of beautiful articles offered for sale: exquisite embroidery, intricate woodcarving, articles in ivory, silver, lapis lazuli, amber and jade. We would be given tea by Suffering Moses 'the worst wood-carver in Srinagar'. To the question why he styled himself thus he would reply: 'Everybody calling himself the best wood-carver in Srinagar. Me, I don't need to boast. Since the great Lord Roberts called me Suffering Moses because he couldn't pronounce my name I have found success and prosperity.' Rested and refreshed we could move to a more energetic life higher up the mountain. Riding ponies which could be hired for 4 annas an hour (1p) we could explore the hillside, climbing through fir forests to the snowline and experiencing moments of choking nostalgia from the sudden vista of a field of buttercups and daisies.

To the east of it was Darjeeling, that fascinating town clinging to the hillside, reached by a mountain railway which must be one of the modern wonders of the world. Here, in contrast to the tall, pale Kashmiris one met the stocky Mongolian types. Each morning rosy-cheeked, cheerful Sikkimese labourers stump into the town laden with fruit and vegetables for the market, the colourful place where one is startled to find oneself served by elegant Lepchu ladies, their black hair worn like a coronet round their heads, their long gowns of fine woollen material cut pinafore style, dark brown over a turquoise blouse or navy blue with cerise, and to protect them aprons of hand-woven striped cloth in many rich colours. From Darjeeling one can look out northward, over the tea gardens on the slopes below, then over a great expanse of forest land to the distant higher range of the Himalayas.

'Where is Kingenjunga?' one asks on the first clear morning, searching for the fabulous peak which is the second highest in the world.

'There!' says our companion, and she is pointing upwards. 'Don't look out, look up!' (We feel there is a parable here somewhere but decide to work it out later.) Then we see it, aloof and majestic, separated from the rest of the range by clouds. Gazing spellbound at the spectacle we whisper: 'It's like a fairy castle in the sky,' using a hackneyed phrase because we cannot think of a better one.

As a change from these and other Himalayan resorts we could go south to the Nilgiris (Blue Mountains) to places with fascinating names like Ootacamund and Coonoor. For me, the excitement would begin on the journey when, once free of the arid northern plains, both the landscape and the people would appear new and interesting. One would be awakened in the morning when the train pulled into a station by the vendor of hot drinks and would be delighted to find coffee pouring from the kettle instead of smoky, milky tea. Unlike our village women of the north, the women and girls boarding the train would be laughing and chattering, their heads uncovered and posies of jasmine tucked into their hair. Idly watching the passing landscape one would suddenly thrill to the sight of a church spire pointing up towards Heaven from the centre of a village or a cross on the gable end of a building, a phenomenon rarely seen when travelling in the north.

The Nilgiris, appearing blue because of the eucalyptus or blue gum trees covering many of the slopes, offer no glorious vista of snow-covered mountains but there are many beauty spots and places of interest. On the Downs above Ooty one met the Todas, a tribe tragically diminishing, distinguished from other aboriginal groups, by their hair style. Both men and women wear their hair in long ringlets and I understand that the ringlets are formed in the same way my mother coaxed my long hair into curls before the 1st World War. The strands of hair are wrapped around half of a long strip of rag, the other half covering it like a bandage and the two ends tied together at the bottom.

Most of these hill resorts which made our annual escape from the burning heat of the plains something to look forward to with pleasure, must have changed in character through the intervening years. Developed by the British for the British in the first instance they now provide holiday venues for a growing number of Indian nationals. Landour, however, does not change so drastically, as it offers no holiday amusements. The most obvious change there today must lie in the diminished number of students in the Language School. Few young people nowadays go to India with a lifetime of service in mind, and short-term volunteers cannot spend time purely in language study but manage to communicate fairly well in English, a language much more widely known and used today.

Three hundred students were attending the school, filling it to capacity that fateful summer of 1938. We saw little of them during the week but on Sundays they crowded into the Union Church or helped to swell the little congregation at the Anglican Church. (A Government-appointed padre served this congregation which was made up of Anglo-Indian boarding housekeepers, and, at that time, a garrison of the Borderers Regiment.) On Saturdays the students took to the hills to climb the neighbouring slopes or to picnic by some waterfall.

It was on my final Saturday that I was invited to join an expedition to Kempti Falls by some young people from the boarding house below ours. We set off in the cool of the morning, pausing to buy fruit from a stall in the Landour bazaar at the bottom of the hill, then walked on to Mussourie, where we stopped for elevenses at the Paris Restaurant, a wooden shack which was the only café in the place in those days, apart from a grand affair in the one hotel. After another three miles down a much steeper mountain road we reached the level of our picnic site. To my horror I found that we were being led across an expanse of huge flat-topped rocks, separated from each other by channels of water. I was already notorious for being clumsy on the feet but an attack of polio in infancy had also left me with the inability to spring. I just could not leap over those channels. It took three of the men to get me across the rocks! Arriving at the Falls I sank under a tree, laughing hysterically but very much bruised and battered. It was Herbert Pritchard of the RBMU who came to my rescue; bringing water to wash my cuts and scratches, then covering them with sticking plaster. As his hands touched mine, it happened. To both of us. Need I say more?

Three days later, Herbert walked with me to the bus terminus. My holiday was over and we were not to meet again until December, when he came from Bihar to spend Christmas with us. He stayed with Alan Neech, later General Secretary of the BCMS and Chairman of the Keswick Council but then a very young missionary living in the same compound. Herbert came triumphantly bringing permission for our engagement from Gordon Guinness, chairman of RBMU. There could be no wedding until he had passed his final exam, hopefully in September, a rule then observed by most missions. So, subject to the approval of my Mission, we planned our wedding for October 1939.

In April Herbert was told that he was free to marry any time he chose. The news seems to have gone to our heads for we decided there and then to be married in Landour in June. By the time I joined Herbert there in late May, preparations were in full swing. Presents began to arrive. Eighty young people in Herbert's boarding house each gave one rupee to a general fund. As there were 18 rupees to the pound, 80 rupees equalled £4.50. I would like to tell you what could be bought for that princely sum in those days. From the Chinese or Indian 'boxwallas' who squatted on their veranda every day after lunch they bought us a beautiful carved table which still stands in our living room; a brass lamp with shade; a luncheon set of 25 pieces of hand-made lace; a set of Chinese embroidered place mats with centrepiece; a set of Chinese silk underwear for me and various smaller articles.

On our second Sunday together we heard a sermon which moved us greatly, sending us after the service, into the wood below the church. Here, sitting on the warm pine needles, we committed our lives, our future life together, afresh to God. I don't remember the sermon but I vividly remember telling the Lord that we would be ready to do whatever He asked of us; to go where He wanted us to go. We were perfectly aware of what that might mean. For one thing, it would mean that we must go willingly wherever the Field Council might ask us to go. We had seen, each in our own Mission, the varying reactions to a suggestion of transfer. The national workers tended to see it as a sign of failure and disgrace and could become bitter and non co-operative. To some of our colleagues it brought dismay and disappointment and we had seen the struggles to be obedient with grace, struggles which were not always victorious.

'We shall be tested on this commitment,' I said as we walked to our boarding houses for lunch. I was remembering how invariably I had returned from a challenging meeting to find myself facing and often being beaten down by severe and adverse circumstances.

The test of our obedience came the next day in the form of a letter from the Mission in London suggesting that we keep to the original plan for an October wedding. I could not be spared from Mirzapur until then.

I will draw a veil over the next two days with their hot, rebellious thoughts. The Lord did eventually lay His cool hand on our hearts, bringing us to acquiescence and peace. And when October came and with it the loveliest, most heart-warming wedding anyone could wish for, we acknowledged that our Father knows best, that all things do work together for good to them that love God, to them who are called according to His purpose.

CHAPTER NINE

The War Years

Our wedding celebration opened on sudden disaster. The blow fell less than twenty-four hours before the time set and it was fortunate that Herbert had already arrived. I was back in my old home in Kachhwa and we were lingering at the lunch table. Even the busy medicals were in no hurry to get away, for Gina had arrived from Madya Pradesh and Connie had come over with me from Mirzapur so there was a great deal of news to hear and to pass on.

'We are about to have an invasion,' said Dorothy who could see the front door from where she sat. 'Dr Everard, Osman and Herbert.'

The three men came into the room looking perturbed, Herbert more than perturbed! He looked distracted and, I think, angry.

'I'm afraid we have bad news for you,' said the doctor, showing me a telegram. 'The Bishop finds that you cannot be married in the new church as it has not been consecrated.'

'Well, of all things!' I exclaimed indignantly. 'At this late hour, what are we going to do?'

A special licence was the answer, of course, then we could be married in the marquee. But who could give us one and how to find such a person in time? 'The Methodist parson in Benares would marry you,' said someone. 'He doesn't need the special licence but he needs three days' notice.' This wasn't much help but Osman was ready with a suggestion.

'You could go back to Mirzapur,' he said. 'The banns have been read out there so Hugh could marry you in that church — just the legal bit. I could drive you over and we would be back by evening and the wedding can go on as planned in this church tomorrow.' He looked at his watch. 'If we leave now we could meet the train coming from C.P. and detach Mr Welch from the rest of the guests and take him with us.'

The plan was hailed with relief and carried out successfully. Rev. Hugh Wallace, bewildered by the sudden invasion, took a little time to satisfy himself that he was right in doing what we suggested and Uncle Welch indignantly refused to give me away clad in travel stained shorts but was supplied with one of Hugh's suits.

No one was about as we went over to the church. Alan Neech opened up the church and called Edith and Mary from the hospital. Neville Everard stood as best man in place of Raymond Goldsworthy who had not yet arrived from the South and I had Gina at my side. So the knot was well and truly tied and, unknown to most of the guests, I was already a married woman when I stepped from the bungalow next morning on the arm of Uncle Welch.

It was a glorious day. The grass was still green after the monsoon rains, the sky was a soft turquoise blue and the scent of the pink and white Vine of Peace climbing the verandah pillars was heavy in the air. The vine matched us in colour for I was in traditional white and my two bridesmaids - Brownie, (who later lost her life in an air crash over Delhi) and Gina were in pink and silver. Our bouquets were of the only flowers in bloom at that season — white roses, white zinnias and sprays of pink gypsophila.

The new church was beautiful. The male nurses had covered the unplastered walls with greenery and, rivalling the flowers for colour, the congregation, 80 per cent Indian, packed the church to the door.

Herbert was waiting for me, looking strange in a dark morning suit. Walter Corlett of the RBMU (who I had first met in the old days at Admiral Stileman's home) beamed at me as I came up the aisle. He was to assist Hugh at the ceremony. The service had been arranged so as to make everyone feel they could take part. The hymn: "Thine forever God of love" we sang in English and "Love divine, all loves excelling" in Hindi. The actual ceremony with the responses was in English but the message was in Hindi.

The guests sat down to lunch in the big marquee, some on seats round the sides, some cross-legged on the matting. Both Indian and English food was served and guests ate what they chose. This was the first time in my experience that British and nationals had eaten lunch together at a European wedding. The norm had been to arrange an Indian meal in some schoolroom while Europeans ate in the bungalow. I think our wedding marked the beginning of a change in missionary/national relationship. We shall always think of this day as our real wedding day. The first ceremony simply fulfilled the demands of the law and meant little to us, the only sweet memory it has left is that of the kindness of our colleagues in our dilemma. The real wedding was a glorious ending to my nine years with BCMS. I thank every one of my colleagues of those years for their love and friendship, for their patience with me during my very silly years, for their fellowship in the gospel. They made my final day among them a day of unclouded happiness.

There could be no thought of a honeymoon for us. The war was only a few days old and nobody knew what might happen. On our way to our new home we spent the night in an unoccupied Mission bungalow which Brownie and Gladys Simm had prepared for us, stocking it with all we needed in the way of food. Unfortunately, the little Christian community took their responsibilities seriously: They prepared tea for us and then sat with us, their children entertaining us with songs and recitations for what seemed like hours. Next morning Herbert and I set out alone to begin our new life together. And because of the war, it was to prove a life of constant change.

Sometimes God allows us to have in full measure that which we have craved and, as it was with the flesh that the Israelites craved in place of the heaven-sent manna, it often sticks in our throats if we have more than enough of it. It was so with me. I had craved change; always looking forward to something which would break the monotony — to Saturday, to the next day of prayer, to the hill holiday, to furlough. Now our lives became too full of change to suit even me. We lived in five different places during the next five years.

Our first home was in Capra. The bungalow had originally stood on the banks of the Gogra, a tributary of the Ganges but the river had moved its course. Now, nine feet below the level of the front lawn, a wide expanse of common land stretched for two miles, land that had become one of the town's lavatories! Over the garden hedge to the left was a temple whose devotees rang the bell and chanted day and night. To the right of us was a narrow street of poorer houses where naked babies crawled in the dust, goats and hens wandered unchecked and dogs yapped or howled throughout the night.

But we were happy as we set up our wedding presents. I remember with gratitude that we needed to buy nothing more than curtains and a clock which was as well for us. Communications had already broken down and no money reached us from London for weeks. There was another of my lurking fears materialising, the fear that for some reason or another the flow of money might stop and leave us stranded at the other side of the world. It was a fleeting fear that popped up its head periodically during the next few years, but which ought to have been slain for ever during those first months of war, banished by the plain fact that God kept His promise and supplied our needs. Although nothing came from London until the following February, none of us suffered hunger. I was even able to make our first Christmas dinner of chicken and plum pudding and, a wonderful treat, we had kippers for breakfast, sent to us by a couple of Scottish people who worked in nearby Norton's sweet factory.

We lived in this house barely three months. John and Margaret whose home it was, fearful of being caught and held up in Britain by the war, cut short their furlough and returned to the field. We packed our new possessions on an oxcart and moved to a preacher's house on the edge of a village. It was rough walled with floors of beaten earth, a 'butt and ben' of a place. In fact, it was the mud hut I had expected to live in when I first arrived in India and with which I had compared unfavourably to our large Saugor bungalow.

The shabby little rooms were soon transformed by the few wedding presents for which we could find room, pretty mats on the floor, pictures on the wall and shining new pans in the kitchen (a lean-to in the back yard!) I sadly cut down our beautiful curtains to fit the small doors and act as purdahs for privacy. Indeed, as we moved from one house to another, each different in size and style, the cutting down and stitching together again of those curtains became for us a symbol of removal.

Four times more over the war years we packed our possessions on the oxcart, the loads a little heavier each time as we were blessed first with a baby daughter and later a son.

'You had better get out here — there's trouble down the line.'

It was one of our colleagues intercepting the train at Motihari and looking very troubled.

'But we can't stop here,' said Herbert. 'I am due in Bina on Friday.'

It was August, 1942, and the "Quit India" uprising had begun. In our remote village on the border of Nepal we had heard vague rumours of trouble beginning in some parts of the country but with that very human optimism which believes that only the other fellow will get it - that it could never happen to us, we had not even considered putting off this visit to my old district in Central Provinces where Herbert was to conduct a Bible school.

We had left home in high spirits. No thought of danger troubled us as we walked along the railroad track in single file. We were quite used to making our exit in this way, for there was no road out of the village in those days. The early morning had been beautiful as monsoon mornings can be. There had been rain in the night and long fingers of black cloud barred the apricot of the dawn sky. High above them, shining palely silver in clear blue hung the crescent moon with her attendant sear. To the south west the sky was still a steel grey over the station buildings and over our heads a huge, white cumulus had caught the light of the still invisible sun and seemed to be illuminated from within with golden light. But the northern horizon behind us had been swept clear of clouds. Several times we stopped and turned to catch another glimpse of the snow-clad Himalayan range visible through the trees, its crystal whiteness tinged with rose. We didn't know that we were not to look upon that scene again for months.

The journey as far as Motihari had been uneventful. At each stop we had taken our two-year-old daughter out for a breath of air and she had evoked the usual smiles which she had come to expect from the crowds thronging wayside stations. And now here was Syd telling us the trouble was serious enough for us to break our journey. We looked around us, everything seemed normal on the platform. Village women ran to and fro like agitated hens, seeking seats on an overcrowded train. Vendors shouted their wares — hot tea, cold drinking, water, cigarettes.

'We heard that a planter had to stand in the doorway of a compartment in Muzaffarpur station and defend two ladies with beer bottles,' Syd was saying. 'You'd better get down now. If the situation improves, you could catch the next train leaving Betty and June here with us.'

There was no next train. The one from which we had alighted never reached Muzaffarpur. Lines had been torn up and thrown into the river. Within hours, every station through which we had passed had been burned to the ground. Had we left by an earlier train it would have carried us beyond our own area into the thick of the trouble and where we might not have found anybody to help us. Had we planned a later train, we would have been trapped in the village, our one exit closed. It could only have been God, our Heavenly Father, who had guided us to that train, and to safety.

We were the first refugees into Motihari. Later in the day, other Europeans were brought in and billeted with British residents. The Bihar Light Horse (BLH), a territorial company from among the planters and Raj officers, constituted themselves our protectors. Each officer became responsible for the Europeans living nearest his home. At the first sign of rioting he was to get his charges to the town jail which had been stocked with emergency provisions.

At breakfast on the Sunday, three days after our arrival, I'd said: 'I wonder how Mr C is? I believe he is alone. I thought of him during my quiet time. I feel rather worried about him.' Mr C, an elderly man, was head of a small mission working to the north of us.

'Could we send a coolie*?' someone asked.

We could, and did so. A servant lad tucked a letter in his cummerbund and set off on a cycle. He returned later that day bringing a message pencilled on our own note. 'Hiding in the fields; am escaping tonight in covered oxcart.'

Syd sent a message to the major of the BLH and he set off immediately with two car loads of men — police and civilians with guns. At the river they looked around and realised that Mr C could not possibly have crossed unaided. The ford was being watched by a mob of students who melted away at the sight of the guns. A boat was commandeered and the party went across — cars and all. A little way along the road they met a cart covered over with a sheet like a cart carrying purdah women.

'That you, brother?' called the major. 'Friends here.'

The purdah was lifted revealing the missionary. He was transferred to the car, given hot coffee and brought to us at the Mission. He was put straight to bed for he was in state of nervous exhaustion. A mob of students from the nearby town had come surging out, determined to take one European life for an Indian who had been shot. They had manhandled him cruelly but during a few minutes when they had left him to consult as the best way to deal with him, his servants had got him away. Friendly villagers had hidden him, first in a barn, and then in one lentil field after another until the students had stopped looking for him. After a few days of rest and quiet he was able to join us at meals. Indeed, he became the leader of the Bible study group we had arranged among ourselves and the Lord gave us a little Keswick in the midst of our fears.

There were reasons for fear. Mobs were roaming the countryside and the compound at Motihari boasted no high wall or barred gates. There were gateposts, but no gates! August being the hottest, stickiest month of the year we couldn't possibly sleep inside closed rooms with no

---

meaning porter (coolie is now considered offensive in USA and Europe)

electric fans to cool the air. We slept on open verandahs and tried to rest on the promise: "Thou shalt not be afraid of the terror by night..."

During my young days, one of the reasons for my shrinking from the thought of service abroad was the fear of finding myself the target of mob violence. My overactive imagination could conjure up visions of myself facing a murderous mob of natives (as we used to call them!) Several times already since my arrival in India I had come near to the actual experience. Word of rioting or uprising somewhere near us would bring on the sudden clutch of fear which always caught me in the stomach and then in the throat. The cause of the rioting might be nothing to do with us but the fact that we were different from everybody else made us an obvious target for people temporarily unhinged. Or so I had imagined. Sometimes during troubled times we were wakened by an abnormally loud clamour of voices. It would turn out to be a false alarm but I would lie awake afterwards, tossing on the hot bed, trying to stop the thoughts going round and round in my head, plans for our escape, wondering which of our neighbours would dare to shelter us. Nothing could break this chain of two o'clock in the morning horrors but a steady reciting of God's promises. "The angel of the Lord encampeth round about them that fear him" and "No evil shall come nigh thy dwelling."

And so it was now when we were nearer to the reality of my nightmare than ever before. Now we were the target. This was the "British Quit India" uprising. Everyday news would come through of trouble in some town, and horrible things were happening here and there. One of our preachers, living in a dangerous place, wrote in red paint on the whitewash of his house, the words running right round the house as the Hindus write the names of their gods:

"The name of the Lord is a strong tower; the righteous runneth into it and is safe."

Any moment, the townspeople of Motihari, the riff-raff and trouble-makers or those who hated Christianity could join with the roving mobs of students and attack us. But each day we found the Word of God quick and powerful as we applied it to our fear.

'Auto-suggestion! something like the Coue system!' you say? Not in the least. Try saying over and over again: 'Nothing is going to happen to me' when the mob is at the gate. See if it will remove your fear. But when you say in your heart: "Lo, I am with you alway," and you believe utterly in the One who said it, you find it is enough. It was in this way that the Lord himself, hungry and weak, repulsed the temptations of Satan.

'But', you say: 'You were not being tempted. You were just a huddle of frightened people trying to assure yourselves that all would be well.'

But we were being tempted — tempted to doubt our Father's care and His power to protect. The reality of our faith was being tested.

It was at midday of one of our most frightening days that I saw this and was greatly strengthened. As we stood round the dining-table waiting for grace, Ruth said: 'Let's sing "God is still on the throne."' She had been talking over the compound hedge with the elderly English lady, mother of a civil servant, who lived next door. In the course of conversation the lady had told Ruth how much she was heartened whenever she heard our singing. 'Let's sing it clearly so that she will be able to hear the words,' said Ruth. To some of us clearly meant loudly! Syd, coming in late, was met by this blast of joyful sound. He had just heard some frightening news and our jubilant singing did something to his nerves.

'You are just being light and frivolous,' he shouted or something to that effect. I can't remember his exact words but coupled with the sight of his white face, they subdued and frightened us. Nothing more was said. The meal progressed in the usual way and it was not until it was over that he told us two mobs were converging on Motihari.

The men gathered together to discuss plans and I went across the lawn to our room. As I put our two- year-old daughter down for her nap, the full force of the horror came upon me. Our cook had just told me that he and the six other servant boys had planned to smuggle June away if anything happened to us, and that piece of information had not helped. My imagination was active again, picturing our precious baby being hidden in some village home, crying for us. Such things had happened in other parts of the world to other babies; lost to everybody but the villagers.

I now saw that this was the reason why my serenity kept breaking down. It wasn't that I didn't believe in God. I believed in Him with all my heart and mind, believed that He was watching us and caring. But I was afraid lest He find it in His purpose to allow us to suffer even violence and death. He had not kept those other children from horror; how could I be sure He would protect ours? He had saved Peter from prison and death by a miracle but he had allowed James to be slain by the sword. All the fear of physical suffering rose to the surface as I sat on my bed by the sleeping child. Was God going to save us from the mob or not? Not could He, but would He? I had to work this thing out now. What I lacked was not so much faith in God as love for Him - the love and loyalty that made Job say: "Though He slay me yet will I trust Him." The love that made Jesus say when faced with unspeakable horror: "Not my will, but Thine be done." I needed enough love for Him to enable me to say and mean it: 'If it is Your will that we go through this, then I'm willing. I know that if You allow us to suffer, even our baby daughter, it will be for Your own good purposes.'

But this needed what I hadn't got — courage. How I needed the courage that Daniel's three friends had when they said to the king who was about to throw them into a burning fiery furnace: "Our God is able to deliver us, and He will deliver us. But if not, know this, oh king! We will not bow down to the golden image." But if not…

Herbert came in at this point. 'There's still no sign of B, he said. (Mr B. was the officer of the Bihar Light Horse appointed to smuggle our party to the jail if danger threatened.) 'It must mean that the rumours we heard were false.'

'Or that Mr B. was not at home,' I replied gloomily. 'He isn't confined to his compound as we are.' Then as the misery rushed over me, I said. 'Oh, I wish we could pick up June and run away!'

'Where would you run?' said Herbert. Then he came and sat beside me on the bed and put his arm around me, comforting me as I poured put all the fears I had had. But he was right. Where could we run but into the powerful, embracing arms of God?

Quietened, I said: 'We're like Peter. When the Lord was so sad as he watched some of His disciples go away because they couldn't bear the hard things He had been saying, He said to Peter "Will you go away, too?" And Peter said: "Where could I go, Lord?"

'Exactly,' said Herbert. 'If we lose our trust in Him, where could we go? He has become everything in the world to us. "Whether we live or die, we are the Lord's."'

That afternoon a handful of British tommies entered Motihari and billeted themselves in the waiting room of the deserted station. Only seven or eight of them, but their presence was enough to dampen the ardour of the mob. Or so it seemed. Gradually the tension eased. More troops arrived and after a while we were allowed to take a short walk and to visit other houses.

The coming of more troops brought also a breath of new life. We had offered to entertain them three evenings a week, arranging games and refreshments and we also hoped to arrange a short epilogue at the end. Mrs H., the first lady of the station, was grateful for the offer and made the planters' wives provide the refreshments seeing that they were willing to entertain only officers. The men who came to us were of the Borderers, mostly North country Englishmen. They played games with great enthusiasm, choosing their teams with a 'me, 'im and 'er. They kept us in constant laughter with their wit and droll fun, especially the Sergeant Major who was a real comic. He told Ruth who came from the Highlands that the only good thing to come out of Scotland was the road to England. And on the first evening when, after accompanying some uproarious community singing, I suggested a few hymns, he said: 'Don't be shy, luv! We've all been to Sunday School.'

Just before Christmas, four months after we had left home, Herbert was allowed to return, but he went under armed escort in an otherwise empty train. He went to see how the Christians had fared in our absence but also to pack our belongings. We had been transferred to Siwan to take the place of Walter and Violet Corlett who had offered to serve with the YMCA in Imphal, Assam, to minister to troops passing to and from the battle front in Burma.

I have described the Quit India uprising as we saw it, but perhaps I should give something of the viewpoint of those who were involved in it. The seething rebellion which made uprising possible in the middle of a desperate war was no new thing. I suppose it had been simmering since the mutiny of 1857 though beneath the surface, erupting now and again in bursts of bitterness and rioting. The modern manifestation, however, could be said to have begun in 1916 when the Indian National Congress, up to then wholly Hindu, was joined by the Muslim Party to begin what was to become a long drawn out crusade for freedom from British rule. About the same time Mr Gandhi came from South Africa and immediately allied himself with them. He soon became a national figure, inspiring all who heard him. Mr Nehru wrote of the influence he exerted and how listening to Mr Gandhi often left him in such a state of mind that he could not go on living the way he had.*

Mr Gandhi became the most formidable opponent of the British Government. He attacked what he thought were the props of British rule — fear, prestige, and the co-operation, willing or unwilling, of the people. He began by encouraging non co-operation, and this culminated in the strikes of 1921. Then he turned to civil disobedience but had to withdraw this as it ended in looting on a massive scale. During the twenties he visited N. Bihar to strengthen the revolt of the farmers against the tyranny of the planters. He organised a march to Bombay to protest against the salt taxes, illegally distilling salt on the beaches, this eventually ended in serious riots (into which ferment I had arrived in 1930). Mr Nehru said Gandhi 'fascinated the masses, attracting them like a magnet'.

When World War 2 began, both Mr Gandhi and the Congress were in a dilemma. Their inherent hatred of oppression made it impossible for them to have sympathy with Japan or Nazi Germany or Fascist Italy. Yet they felt that the British could not be said to be fighting for liberty and democracy when they steadily refused to let India go free. According to Mr Nehru, there was

---

* From 'Discovery of India' written by Nehru during his imprisonment 1942 to 1946

*Elizabeth (Betty) Fazackerly
with her parents and brother.*

Early days in Central India. In 'camp' with the Biblewomen.

Travelling by Ekka.

First meeting at the picnic at Mussourie; (Herbert in the foreground with Betty holding a cup).

The 'official' wedding day 12th October 1939.

Lillia and Sudhan (co-workers).

Herbert and Betty with June and Michael.

Betty wrote Sunday School manuals which were used across India and also in other countries.

Herbert and Betty enjoying retirement.

widespread bitterness in the country as it was forced into a War that wasn't its concern. There was a small group who even felt that it could take advantage of a Japanese invasion to free India. This group was prepared to do anything to hinder the War effort. (This was one reason why, in the uprising of 1942, we had more trouble in our area than in many other parts of the country. We were in the direct line of communication with the battle front; trains were passing through our district day after day, carrying troops to Burma.)

On the other hand, while ineffectual efforts to induce Britain to negotiate had made the freedom fighters desperate, the masses had become apathetic, dumbly waiting whatever events might happen.

Mr Gandhi therefore insisted that something must be done to rouse the people, some blow struck now for freedom. He saw that, whether the War was won or not, this submissive spirit would put freedom further away than ever.

The Congress was unwilling to do anything to embarrass Britain when the War was at its most desperate stage. They believed that if the effort to resist a Japanese invasion were hindered and some eastern area occupied, there would be a breakdown of civil administration over a wide area, leading to chaotic conditions. Finally, however, wearied by Britain's constant refusal to make any agreement with them, in August 1942 the Congress drew up what came to be known as the Quit India Resolution. After putting forward arguments for the immediate freeing of India they stated that they could 'no longer feel justified in holding the nation back from endeavouring to assert its will against an Imperialistic and autocratic Government. The Council resolves therefore to sanction for the vindication of India's inalienable right to freedom and independence, the starting of a mass struggle on non-violent lines under the leadership of Mr Gandhi.'

A few hours later, in the early hours of August 9th, the British authorities having become aware of this, a large number of arrests were made all over the country and the Quit India period had begun.

For a movement organised by desperate people, there was not a tremendous amount of bloodshed. This was accredited to Mr Gandhi's doctrine of Ahimsa (non-violence) but there were other factors. During the time — three weeks, I think — before Britain could get troops to the danger areas, it was the courage and loyalty of the civil authorities and police, British and national, which curbed the fury of the mobs that were out, not for passive resistance, but for blood.

In time, the dangerous situation eased. The leaders, Mr Nehru, Mr Gandhi, Mr Jinnah and others were in prison and on the surface peace prevailed. But it was only a truce. The granting of independence was just round the corner and there was to be much more bloodshed before it was finally established.

CHAPTER TEN

Change

Many of the changes wrought by the war were not distressing but added to our comfort. For instance, we saw the end of the tyranny of the topi. We had been forced to wear this unbecoming, helmet-like headgear whenever we left the house and at every hour of the day. Woe betide the young recruit caught crossing the garden without its protective covering. She could wear it at whatever angle she pleased, over one eye or on the back of the head, but wear it she must.

I believe it was the British Army that pronounced its doom. The powers that be had decided to risk sending the troops to India without topis. This was in the nature of an experiment, exposing the men to the dangers of sunstroke — being hit with the 'Deolali stick' in the soldiers' jargon! — and the number of casualties from exposure to the sun was found to be no more than before. The power of the topi was broken.

It was a good thing. As the fashion for wearing it waned among Europeans so it ceased to be a status symbol among the Christian brethren. Preachers of the less humble type had tended to wear it as a sign of their superior position when it simply marked them as outsiders who sucked up to Britain. The preacher whom we had left behind during the Quit India period, bravely trying to carry on his evangelism during our absence, made the mistake of appearing in the bazaar in a topi. It was immediately knocked from his head and kicked to a pulp. I don't think he ever bought another – indeed they soon disappeared from the shops.

I must say that I have always been thankful that Indian Christian women have had the good sense to hold on to their elegant national dress though at that time a few Biblewomen still appeared looking like Edwardian ladies in voluminous, floor-length skirts and full-sleeved blouses. Brides, too, were often dressed in the style of their western sisters, even to the wearing of gloves. I have a vivid memory of myself leaving the organ and going to the rescue of a bride who could not pull the kid glove from her perspiring hand. So long were we in the process that the town band, hired for the occasion, grew impatient and struck up 'Yes, we have no bananas' at the most serious part of the ceremony!

Looking back I realise that the war shattered many stuffy notions and rules which made life intolerable and often fatal for a previous generation of women. The shattering process had begun with the First World War but fragments still remained among us. My generation of missionaries had escaped by a few years the horror of Edwardian styles but there were ladies still among us who knew what it was to endure tight lacing, high, well boned collars, long sleeves and skirts that swept up the dust of India while the temperature soared to 120 F in the shade. Though we were more fortunate we still suffered from remnants of the British dogged determination to conform to home standards however unsuitable they might be to the climate and culture of a foreign country.

The proverbial Englishman not only went out in the midday sun but he ate his lonely dinner in his tent deep in the jungle, perspiring in dress shirt and tie. But he did it to keep up the standard of life he thought right and decent, to discipline himself and to prevent himself from letting go and going native.

We would have denied that we were suffering certain discomforts for the sake of British prestige. We believed we were motivated only by a desire to cause no offence to the people to whom we had been sent. We would suffer any discomfort rather than let our manner of dress cause someone to despise our message and turn away from Christ.

We women wore stockings, for instance, lisle thread or cotton though at times we could have wept as we drew them over limbs running with perspiration five minutes after a cool bath. I had been a rebel against this unnecessary burden from the beginning and during my second year I believed we had proved the futility of it.

Amy and I were in camp. One day, picnic lunch over, we started off for another village and found a jungle stream in our way. The Biblewomen leapt over nimbly and held out hands to Amy and me, both notably clumsy about the feet. We jumped together. There was a splash behind me as I scrambled up the bank. Amy had fallen into the water.

'That settles it,' she said, peeling off her stockings and grimacing as she thrust her feet into the wet shoes. 'We'll have to go home. I can't sit in a village without stockings.'

'Why not? The Biblewomen do,' I said and glanced enviously at their bare, brown feet in open sandals. 'Your dress is almost as long as a sari.'

It was undeniably long. Since we often had to squat on the ground we had been careful to wear longish, full dresses however unfashionable they might be. 'Look', I went on as she shook her head doubtfully. 'Now is our chance to prove whether or not the villagers will be shocked. You can sit on the wall (the low stone walls were our best pulpits) and talk to them while I watch the women and see if anyone is diverted by your bare ankles.'

Nobody was, of course. In fact, we were freed from the embarrassing attention often paid to our stockings by the children sitting at our feet as they tried to see how the fascinating articles were anchored; or pulled at them gently, murmuring 'rub-b-ber?'.

But back in the compound our gleeful report made no difference. Prejudice and preconceived ideas do not give way easily before arguments. Notions we have grown up with die hard. To be seen in the streets of Britain without stockings would be a shocking thing, therefore it must be equally shocking in an Indian village.

We were not really rebels at heart. We tried to give in gracefully but all that we had desired was that any sacrifice of our comfort we were asked to make might be logical and reasonable. The disapproval which kept us from cutting our long hair did have some significance, for the Hindus crop the hair of widows. It is a sign of humiliation and degradation so one could see that the villagers might be repelled at the sight of a bobbed or shingled head. But bare, sandaled feet had no significance at all.

We must have been convinced in our minds that to keep the peace and guard the fellowship was more important than getting our own way. The era of defiance and open rebellion among the young had not yet dawned. We continued to bear the discomforts cheerfully until the war years changed public opinion. In the subtle way a fashion has of becoming commonplace that practically everybody accepts it, the comfort of short hair and sandaled feet became permissible to all of us.

This secondary matter of outward appearance never again recaptured the important place it had held in people's thinking. Looking back I have been saddened at the power it has had to tear apart the body of Christ, to promote conflict between Christians of one thought and another. The more conforming among us have been tempted to find in it a justification for giving way to a critical and judging spirit while the devil has used it to tempt young people to rebellion, a sin which is surely more grievous to the Lord than is the flouting of conventional patterns.

And it is a secondary matter as we were reminded one evening during a language school get-together in Landour. A discussion on mission had been arranged with Dr Stanley Jones in the chair. Opinions were being aired about our witness, whether or not it could be more effective if we dressed in national costume, lived in smaller houses and ate national food. Suddenly one of the national teachers provoked no doubt by this display of tactless superiority, rose and said passionately: 'We don't care what sort of houses you live in. We know those of you who love us and understand us.'

How right he was. A few weeks later I was standing at the door of the outpatients department waiting for the doctor. A very old lady who could remember the Mutiny of 1857 and still spoke lovingly of "Wictoria Rani" was standing beside me. She was a regular attender at outpatients, being sent whenever a purdah woman was ill. She stood now looking me over with a quizzical expression, from my feet, along my bare arms and to the lowish neck of my dress.

'I remember the days,' she croaked, 'when the Memsahib log* wore dresses up to here and down to here – and here,' and she pointed from her chin down to her wrist and finally to the dust at our feet.

'Did you like it better that way?' I asked gently.

She nodded – then her old eyes twinkled in her wrinkled face. 'Aray, no!' she said. She smiled at me and patted my bare arm. I knew she loved me and she knew I loved her, and nobody listened more readily than she to my words about Jesus.

Living as we now were in the remote villages of North Bihar we were spared many of the horrors of the war, the terror of falling bombs, of blasted buildings, wrecked homes and mutilated bodies. Nevertheless, though we seemed to be far from the turmoil, it was working its changes in our lives quietly, as surely as it was breaking up the ordered pattern of life in the West.

We were not aware of it at first. The changing relationship between foreign missionary and national Christians, for instance, was so slow that we were long in recognising it. It was inevitable that the Christian community should be affected by the unrest, the anti-British spirit which still worked like yeast under the surface of Indian life. Everybody knew that Independence was just around the corner. As soon as the war was over the British would leave India for ever – including the missionaries. Of this latter exodus the Christians seemed to have no doubt.

The effects of this assumption varied. The ordinary Christians were dismayed and frightened, just as the prospect of British withdrawal dismayed and frightened the ordinary villagers. And as there were, all over India, men who saw for themselves a place of power in the new India, so there were, here and there, ambitious Christians who saw themselves as future leaders of the Christian community and began to plan accordingly. Sadly, as was afterwards proven, the ambition was not always to assume a spiritual leadership; that had been open to them for years. Control of mission funds and property was an alluring prospect and because the motive was ulterior, the means of attaining it were devious and underhand.

Nevertheless, God was using the situation to produce a spirit of independence among a people who had been dependent on foreign missionaries for far too long, and so to bring into

---
* folk

birth the self-supporting, self-governing, self-propagating church for which we had prayed and worked. Perhaps it was because we were tired and strained that we failed to perceive this at the time but were conscious only of the distresses, the embarrassments of the first niggling birth-pangs.

The pain became almost intolerable during the first two years of war. Details of that period are hazy in my memory. Trying to sort out events is like groping in a mist. It is as if my mind had rejected them, tearing them out of memory's album like embarrassing photographs. I have only a confused recollection of physical exhaustion; of interminably hot days when it seemed as if the sun would never go down; of a sense of isolation; of undercurrents of hostility in the compound; of bitterness in the hearts of a beloved people; of treachery never revealed openly but masked behind smiles and apparently warm fellowship; of a sickening suspicion that all was not well morally with the teachers and the older boys of the school to which we were attached. Yet when I try to pierce the darkness and confusion I see one or two pictures, sharp in detail like cameos laid on dark velvet.

It was our final camp of the winter. Leaving the problems of the compound for a while we had pitched out tent on the outskirts of a village. I see us sitting cross-legged on the mat of the prayer-tent at the end of the day — Aza and her Biblewomen, two preachers, our cook, our two children and ourselves. Leading us in prayer is the man whose love and loyalty had cheered us through the troubled days. P. was a Brahmin who had been led to the Lord by Walter Corlett a few years before and we had watched his growth in grace and joy. Now in the camp when his turn came round to lead us in worship we were not only blessed and uplifted but also astonished at his grasp of deep, spiritual truths. His messages were refreshingly alive, his spiritual maturity impressive. It was maturity that had grown with suffering.

His family, and indeed the whole village, had bitterly opposed his turning to a new faith. After his baptism he was forced to leave his home but over and over again he returned to seek reconciliation. On these occasions his Mother would nor refuse him food; that would be against all the Hindu laws of hospitality, but she would feed him in the way she would feed a passing beggar – outside the door. Once he was sure that she had put poison in his food. He went out of the village and was violently sick and he always affirmed that it was the Lord who had caused him to vomit and so get rid of the poison.

He had come to live in the compound, accepting a job that, to a Brahmin, was degrading, an outcast's job, and because of his integrity, his intelligence and capability he had risen to be head of the carpentry school. Then he had known persecution from brethren who should have been rejoicing in his conversion, watching his growth with delight as we were. It was a petty persecution, rooted perhaps in the jealousy of his cultured background, his ability to preach and to open up the word of God. There could have been resentment because of his loyalty to us or perhaps it was the fact that he walked with God, calm and seemingly unaffected by the distemper of those around him.

The sad part of the picture is that when persecutions began to touch his new wife, he wasn't willing to bear it. He left the district shortly after our departure for furlough and became a pillar of the church in another province. Only the day when all the books are opened and hidden things laid bare will it be revealed just how much the church in our area was set back by his rejection and his going from us.

I see another picture. In the corner of the office, seated facing each other on a straw mat, are my husband and a local farmer. The large Hindi Bible is open on the man's lap and his finger is marking the place. Astonishingly, the place is the eighth chapter of Romans and the man is listening to Herbert with a rapt look on his intelligent face. He too is a Brahmin. His home is in P's village. He had appeared one day and asked to be taught about the Christian religion.

'I have watched P. since he became a Christian,' he explained. 'I watched him when he was stoned and I saw nothing of anger in him at any time. He never once attempted to defend himself, never took up a stone. He still visits his family and although they no longer throw stones they still hate him. Even his mother. And he meets their hate with nothing but love. I want to know his secret.'

It was April and the rice was harvested. There was no work in the fields. Could he not stay in the compound and learn? He could and did, and we loved his enthusiasm. Then one day he asked to be baptised. He had counted the cost. That same afternoon he went to the bazaar to buy some stores (we had not allowed him to break his caste by eating with us before he had made up his mind to become a Christian). He didn't return that evening and he has not been seen by anyone since. Someone had been determined that the Brahmins of that village should not be shamed again.

My next picture is clearest of all. It is the one memory for which I had no need to grope. It was the time I came to terms with my affliction of deafness. This had been troubling me since the birth of our first child and was becoming steadily worse. I was beginning to realise with dismay that it was no temporary discomfort but something that had come to stay.

It was Conference week. We were gathered together from all parts of the district and as usual had begun with a day of prayer and fellowship. Throughout the long morning session I had sat in frightening silence, hearing nothing but the prayer of Mama Banks who was kneeling beside me. (We knelt in prayer in those days.) After lunch, Herbert and Ruth Horne came into the little room we had set aside as the nursery and found me weeping as I fed the baby – weeping tears of self-pity.

Moved by the Lord (as I am sure we were) we three came together to pray for my healing. We told the Lord that we believed absolutely in His power to heal me. We believed that He could perform this miracle in answer to our fervent prayers. He didn't need the help necessarily of those specially endowed with the gift of healing. His was the power, not ours. We were conscious of the presence of the Lord in that little room. We knew we had been heard. Yet all the time the words were repeating themselves in my mind – "My grace is sufficient for you, for my strength is made perfect in weakness" – the answer God gave to the apostle Paul when he pleaded three times for deliverance from his thorn in the flesh. And I was not sure whether this was the voice of God telling me that there was to be no sudden miracle, or whether it was simply the association of ideas – Paul's thorn and my ears. But I kept on asking Him in my heart how I could grow in grace and knowledge if I remained shut out from people's prayers and messages.

The first hymn of the afternoon session brought a rebuke. It was "Oh for a thousand tongues to sing my great Redeemer's praise". As I opened the book, one line stood out as if it were in heavier type – **hear Him, ye deaf.** The second hymn was startling in its underlining of the message to me. "Open my ears that I may hear, messages of truth Thou sendest clear."

In that meeting, I knew the truth and accepted it. For some purpose of His own God was not going to give me back my hearing. I didn't know what that purpose might be – I was to get a glimpse of it in later years, but in the meantime I was to go forward and prove that the grace available to each of us in our times of weakness and stress really is sufficient. Our next period of service, the work to which we returned after furlough was to test this grace to the utmost.

Furlough, when it came, to me after eight long years, to Herbert after seven, was a time of mixed happiness and trouble, difficulty and delight. It began in Preston in the late afternoon of a bitterly cold and snowy January Sunday, 1945. Light from the hall of my home shone out across the snow, warm and welcoming, as my mother opened the door and stood for a moment staring at us in astonishment. 'Well now, look who's here!' she cried; then recovering ushered us into the living room. The tea things were still on the table, my father was in his usual chair facing the door and my brother's two children were sitting cross-legged on the rug before the fire. Our four-year-old daughter, always friendly and uninhibited, smiled at her cousins and joined them on the rug. Michael, now eighteen months old, walked straight across to my father, leaned against his knee and gazed up at him solemnly and confidently.

Herbert was bringing in the baggage. 'Leave it in the hall,' I said, 'and come and meet the family.'

My parents were now recovering from the shock of our unexpected arrival. There followed a confusion of noise, of exclamations and laughter, greetings and introductions. My father was having difficulty in peeling off Michael's coat.

'What do you call this?' he ejaculated and held the small green garment up by the shoulders. Held like this the sleeves stood out at an angle like small drainpipes! Everybody laughed except my mother who was coming from the kitchen with fresh cups and saucers.

'E-e-eh!' she exclaimed. 'Poor little lad!'

I felt choked with emotion for a moment. It had been so long since I had heard that north country sound that usually precedes some emotional ejaculation. I had forgotten, too, my mother's capacity for seeing pathos in the thing that was amusing everybody else.

'The coats were made by the derzi* — from blankets,' I said. 'What else could we do?'

What indeed? The children had been born during the war years when no parcels had come from Britain. My own coat had also been made from a blanket. It fitted better than Michael's but it too was green, entirely the wrong colour as I was to find out the first Sunday in church where it stood out like a sore thumb amid the sober browns, navy blues and blacks! The coats-from-blankets had seemed a marvellous notion up there on the Mussourie hills. Quite a number of missionaries were resorting to this way out of a difficulty now that the war was coming to an end and furloughs were a possibility.

They should pass muster in the shabby Britain the BBC newscasters had led us to expect. But nothing had appeared shabby to us as, during the long journey from Glasgow where we had docked, we searched the crowds on the platforms. Not a pair of clogs did we see though we had been led to believe that many people had been reduced to wearing them. We did see some fur coats! I'd already begun to regret the shabby clothes that had taken up so much room in our baggage and which would never see the light of day in well-dressed Britain.

At the tea-table we apologised for our unheralded arrival. 'We weren't allowed to send a cable,

---

* *local tailor*

not even a wire from Glasgow. Our ship was bringing home Wingate's famous Chindits – the regiment that made such a name for itself on the Burma front. We would have been a fine target for the Japanese had they known.'

The voyage had been the most uncomfortable we had ever experienced. The ship was still a troop-ship, less than half of it converted roughly into some semblance of civilian accommodation. Men passengers slept in dormitories, women and children shared cabins on another deck. Thus the mothers were for most of the time responsible for the children. Many of us slept in our day clothes, haunted by the fear that we might be late on deck if an alarm should sound in the night. Each evening I fell into a troubled sleep after rehearsing over and over what I must do if this happened. First shake the children awake and set June dressing herself while I pulled on the baby's warm clothes, then pick up the bag containing a bottle of water and a packet of food (supplied by the ship). Then up three flights of stairs and several steep hatchways, three lifebelts slung over one shoulder and the baby over the other, following the green arrows to our appointed lifeboat station. And only seven minutes allowed.

I remember with gratitude the kindness of a young girl who shared my cabin after Port Said (along with three Anglican nuns). She was a dancer and had been out east with ENSA, entertaining the troops. She was out of her bunk at the slightest whimper from Michael for she knew how I worried if the children disturbed the nuns.

I remember our surprise and delight when the majority of passengers turned up for the service of hymn singing we had arranged along with some CIM missionaries who had escaped from China. We found that the most irreligious seeming, worldly people chose hymns such as "What a Friend we have in Jesus" and "Tell me the Old, Old Story". And how they sang!

I remember the kindness of the harassed officers and crew in preparing a Christmas party for us. It was a splendid dinner even though we ate it from bare tables. Then there were the not-so-dark evenings when, the children in bed, we would slip through the blackout curtains on the deck and, leaning on the rail, would watch the comforting shapes of the convoy ships that were escorting us home.

Furlough for people with small children is not necessarily a time of unclouded happiness. With no home of one's own to come to, dependent on the hospitality of parents no longer young, one is conscious of being a burden, especially when, as it was in our case, there seems to be no possibility of renting a place of one's own. Deputation work also brings its difficulties. In the early days of our furlough this took on almost nightmare proportions for we felt that we had nothing but heartache and failure to share with supporters who had faithfully upheld us over the difficult years.

I remember that we had been home but a couple of months or so when we had to speak at the Mission's Spring Meetings in London. In the room behind the platform, we met again Elizabeth Franklin who had been with us for the past two years. She was still looking haggard and drawn. We looked at each other and said: 'What have we to say?'

I was able to join Herbert in only one more period of deputation. He was working from the London area and we stayed at the Mission's headquarters, Homelands, a lovely house in Upper Norwood which had been the Children's Home until the war scattered the children. There was ample room for all of us and a spacious garden for the children to play in. Here we enjoyed the fellowship of John Pritchard and his wife just before he left England to become principal of the

Auckland Bible College, New Zealand, and with many of our colleagues from other countries. Here, too, we almost lost our little girl. Rushed to Croyden Hospital with appendicitis, she was on the operating table at noon but was still unconscious in the evening, a doctor sitting by her bed. I was told to send for my husband who was in Wales. Wartime conditions meant only emergency telegrams. I had to state plainly — June dying. Come at once — before they would send the wire. Everybody at Homelands began to pray. Ellen Hall phoned the Chilvers. Cyril, just leaving for his prayer meeting, got his people praying. Herbert, crossing England through the night, claimed healing for June. We were at her bedside early next morning and found her awake. A nurse beamed at us. 'I think God has answered your prayers.' We hadn't told her we had prayed.

Then there was VJ Day when after a happy time introducing the family to Mount Hermon College staff, I went with Miss Crocker to the City to see the celebrations. We sat on the grass outside Buckingham Palace waiting for the Royal Family to come out on to the balcony. I never again had such a close and intimate time of fellowship with the beloved principal who is now with the Lord.

And there was, of course, an introduction to Ulster which has been my home ever since. Here among Herbert's people I found a warm welcome and made many friends whose love and care for me and mine has lasted to this day. I loved Ulster's people and I loved Ulster — its marvellous coastline, its quiet loughs, the unexpected vistas of mountains at the end of the poorest streets. Although as I write the Troubles are still raging, I would not choose to be in any other place.

CHAPTER ELEVEN

In a Medical World Again

'Here comes the pilot!'

The shout brought a general move of passengers to the ship's rail from where we could watch the launch skimming over the calm waters of Port Said harbour, always an exciting event. I had already had my usual thrill, a thrill that the first glimpse of the water-front at this port always gave me. On each outward journey, the palm trees, the dazzlingly white buildings, the suddenly warm air and gentle breeze were a foretaste of the life to which we were going — the mysterious East. When homeward bound, tired and jaded as we were, Port Said spelled the end of the sight and smells of the East, the heat, the dirt and the flies, the poverty and the squalor for ahead of us were the cool waters of the Mediterranean and beyond them home.

On this December morning in 1946 we were on our way back to India. It was a beautiful morning, the sea like watered silk, a soft grey, shot with blue, purple and a lovely pellucid green. A little way from us a young girl was holding our six-year-old daughter as she stood on the bottom rail. They were both singing softly:

"Do you want a pilot? Signal then to Jesus.
Do you want a pilot? Bid Him come on board.
For He will safely guide across the ocean wide
Until we reach at last the Heavenly Harbour."

We watched until the launch drew to the side of the ship, put off the pilot who climbed nimbly up the rope ladder then disappeared. As soon as we docked we would go ashore for a while and I knew exactly what would happen. The vendors of curios and trinkets, Turkish delight and picture postcards would impede our walk at every step. The perfume sellers would walk alongside us, pleading persistently: 'Oh, Mrs McKenzie! (they seemed to call all passengers by this name), Mrs McKenzie! Sniff this one. I give you one sniff last you a lifetime.'

Shaking them off, we would wander toward the shops, the smell of warm dust strange in our nostrils. We would spend a pleasant hour in the huge store of Simon Artz, not buying — just looking. Perhaps we might take a cup of coffee for the fun of the thing, then back to the ship where the children would join others squatting on deck watching with round eyes the manoeuvres of the Gili-Gili man as he brought forth his coloured scarves, his blue love-birds and numerous chickens from the pockets or the ears of slightly nervous youngsters.

'I'll go and see if there is any mail for us,' said my husband as Egyptian officials began to come on board. 'Wait for me on this deck.'

I turned from the busy scene on the dockside and leaned over the rail, looking seaward. I watched the vendors of brightly coloured mats and bags keeping their balance on the swaying boats far below us. They were throwing ropes up to passengers and tying wares to the other end to be drawn up for inspection. But my mind was only half with them. I was feeling a sudden rush of gratitude to God for this unexpectedly comfortable journey. Apparently ours was the first India-bound liner after the War to be fitted out once again as a passenger ship.

I turned as Herbert touched my arm. He had letters in his hand and there was a strange look on his face.

'What is it?' I asked quickly.

He leaned on the rail beside me. 'We're not going to Raxaul,' he replied. 'We are asked to proceed to Gopalganj.'

'Why are missionaries always asked to proceed and never just simply to go?' I asked flippantly. But I said it to cover my dismay. We had been looking forward so eagerly to a new life in Raxaul. In Gopalganj we would be working on the other side of the river again, separated from most of our colleagues who would be a twenty-four hour journey away. 'Why must we go there? Hadn't we suffered enough on that side of the river?'

'Why is this being asked of us,' I said.

'Nani (an elderly missionary already retired) is alone there and the police are giving trouble; they are squatting in the old office buildings,' said Herbert, and added rather bitterly. 'We're to go and guard the property!'

He was looking terribly distressed and I was glad that the young girl had moved away with June. 'Mr Vine must think it necessary,' I said tentatively. Horrible things had been happening all over India while we had been away. Independence had not yet been granted because the Muslim leader was insisting on a partition of the country while the Hindu Congress was desperately opposing it. Fighting had broken out, not straight fighting but the massacre of whole communities and the burning of whole villages. 'Perhaps the compound is really in danger,' I added.

I was only trying to soften the blow, to quell the mutinous thoughts that had gripped us but it was the sort of soft answer that tends to inflame rather than to turn away wrath!

'Where is the will of the Lord in this?' said Herbert. 'We're simply being sent for convenience as caretakers! Well, we're not going.'

We stood looking out over the blue-green sea, seeing nothing. We were both remembering (as we found out later) that Sunday morning seven years before when we had sat on the pine-covered hillside below the church in Landour and committed ourselves wholly to the will of God for our lives and how that commitment had been tested. We recalled how sorry we had been for the bitter words we had spoken, the rebellious feelings we had entertained for longer than we cared to recall because we were being thwarted. But now we were a little further on in our Christian pilgrimage. We had learned by sorrowful experience how the root of bitterness if allowed to remain and to sprout even in one heart can, as the writer to the Hebrews puts it, defile many. We had been learning the wisdom of immediately handing over to God the hurt feelings, the resentments, the self-pity before they can begin their deadly work in the heart. So although this present disappointment was far more crushing than the other had been it did not trouble us for so long. We were able to tell the Lord that we still trusted Him with our future and to join the children for the trip ashore with a measure of enjoyment.

The railway platform at Harkhua, jumping-off place for Gopalganj, was not very crowded. As we stepped from the train a coolie came forward to help us drag out our boxes and bedding rolls. This done he wound his Puggaree cloth into a tight pad on the top of his head and with Herbert's help hoisted a trunk on to it, then stood awaiting orders. We looked around for a welcome face but there was none, only curious eyes that stared solemnly at the children. We had not been met: always before there had been someone; missionary colleagues, Nationals, or a line of grinning schoolboys. The crowd followed us and watched as our baggage was stacked on two 'Ekkas' (the table-top contraptions mentioned earlier) and we climbed on to another. The three more active members of the family sat cross-legged, facing forward, while I dangled my legs over the side. There was no back rest. If I'd known that we still had three miles to cover seated on this horrible cart I would have sat down in the road and wept! After three days travel from Bombay this was the proverbial last straw. The children were enchanted with this new style of locomotion. Michael, now aged three, slid forward to sit nearer the driver who was perched on the shafts, (this is a necessary arrangement for otherwise the horse would have been lifted off his feet by our weight behind) and pretended to drive the poor knock-kneed beast.

Once out of the station road we gathered a little speed, lurching in and out of potholes, passing an endless line of bullock carts, all going the same way, all empty. They had brought sugar cane from distant villages to the sugar mill near the station and were now on their leisurely way home. On the outskirts of the town we passed the Government Hospital which looked surprisingly clean and spacious in its grassy enclosure; the Treasury where the armed sentry watched us pass without curiosity. We had to weave our way through the crowds still thronging the law courts. Then just as I flinched at the thought of passing through the crowded bazaar with its staring multitudes we swerved sharp left and were on the road to the Mission. This narrow dirt road takes a straight course across the country-side. It is a raised road because of floods and at no place is it bordered by hedges. We could see away across the fields on either side, fields of young wheat shimmering silver in the evening light, patched here and there by the dark green of a lentil plot. The sun was setting on our left and even as we watched it dipped below the horizon. Toddy palms stood out black against the pale sky and the wheat changed from glittering silver to a soft, glowing green. The evening was windless. Wood smoke rose from every hamlet and hovered over it like a benevolent cloud. A delicious aroma of baking chippatees came to our noses as we passed wayside huts. Mist-like clouds of dust hung over the road in places, left by the shuffling feet of home-going cattle.

I gave a sigh of relief as the peace of evening seeped into me. We were to live in the real country once again. Here the sounds of the town, a menacing, evil sound would not come to drive me from the veranda into the shelter of the house as they had done in our last station. We met nobody as we passed through the compound and up to the house. Here we were greeted by the elderly lady who had already retired and would soon be leaving for home.

'They didn't bring out the town band for us, did they?' said Herbert, smiling, as we sat drinking tea and eating surprisingly good cake made from coarse brown flour.

'Who?' the lady asked.

'The Christians.'

She smiled back at him. 'You'll find they're just shy.'

'I hope she's right,' I remarked a little later when, the grimy children bathed and bedded, we were making up our own beds.

'In what?'

'In that the folk here are just shy. I'd hate to think we were facing anti-British feelings again.'

'We'll give them the benefit of the doubt,' said Herbert, and with that wise remark he began the unpacking.

In the bright light of morning, the house looked shabby and dreary. The walls needed a new coat of whitewash and the windows couldn't have been cleaned for months. The furniture, bought with the bungalow at the turn of the century from departing Indigo planters, was old and ugly. The large dining-table had split down the middle, the wood probably warping during the monsoons or from lack of oil in the dry heat. And everywhere I could see what had been my pet abomination in India - small tables, stools and wall shelves made from rough unpolished or unpainted wood that time and dust had reduced to a greyness matched only by the greyness of the polished cement floors. (I discovered later that once the sweeper had been persuaded to wipe these floors every day with a damp cloth instead of simply sweeping with a besom, they began to shine like polished black marble!)

There was no running water. Every drop had to be pumped by hand or drawn from the well. We had no refrigerator to keep food cool and clean and the nearest shop was two miles away. Even if we had owned a fridge we could not have used it for electricity had not yet come that way and kerosene oil was strictly rationed. We needed every drop for the lamps by the light of which we read or worked at night. The larder was a small cupboard – four-and-a-half feet high and two feet wide, with fine wire mesh let into door and sides for air. I opened the door and large black ants, suddenly disturbed, scuttled out of the sugar basin. I glanced down. The four earthenware pots in which the 'doolie' stood and which should have been full of water to act as a sort of moat over which the ants couldn't cross, were dry.

But when I went outside, my spirits rose again; the January mist had disappeared before the rising sun which was now turning the dewdrops on every blade of grass into jewels, and shining through the petals of the few poppies in the strip of garden until they glowed like rubies. To the left was a small grove of mango trees with pineapple plants at their feet. The whole compound was surrounded by a hedge of custard apple, and here and there were banana and papaya trees. I had already seen the large kitchen garden at the back of the house and rejoiced in the thought of its possibilities. There would be no lack of fruit and vegetables.

Although the Christians of Tirbirwa (as our village was called) later became our dearest friends and helpers, getting to know them took time. The old paternalistic system had lingered longer here than in most places and they had always held their foreign missionaries in awe and reverence. I think they found our efforts at fraternal friendship embarrassing and held themselves aloof. They certainly misinterpreted our determination to treat them as adults and not as children to have everything done for them. We were to them these 'hard young missionaries'. For instance, it took months of Herbert's consistent refusal to repair the roof of the old Mission 'Godown' which they had been using as a church before they began to move toward building a place of worship of their own. It took another year of steady refusal on his part to take up the sole responsibility of supervising the building of it before they roused themselves to build what became a worthy little church of their own.

The missionaries who had founded this station at the turn of the century were Victorians and they had maintained it in the spirit of Benevolent Victorians. The welfare of the Christian community had been their consideration almost above everything else. They had cared for them in sickness and guarded their affairs in health. They had fed and clothed them when necessary, educated them, found jobs for them, arranged the children's schooling, and written all business letters for them. They had preached to them each Sunday and gathered their children for Sunday School.

For instance, on our first Sunday I asked our elderly colleague about arrangements for Sunday School and was told that there had been none since the last missionary left. 'I have not been well enough to do it,' she said.

'But' I protested, 'surely Lillia could have gathered the children with her own and given them a lesson?'

She was immediately on the defensive, 'They can't do what we do; they haven't the stamina.'

A few years later this same young mother was running her own department in a crowded dispensary and was in complete charge of our leprosy work. It was she who supervised the building of the church, revealing herself an astute business woman as well as a person of strong character and an intelligent and able co-worker.

The old paternalistic approach to missionary work carried with it, of course, all the prestige that used to belong to the manor house, the equivalent of the cap-doffing and curtseying of a vanished era at home, and therefore it created the same gap in relationships. For all the love and devotion and self-sacrifice of the 'Sahibs' they had not allowed even the most respected of their people to go beyond the veranda, or the office. A cup of tea might be sent out to a preacher but he was never invited to sit at the dining table. Nor, in many cases, had the missionary eaten with them. One elderly person who lived with us for a short time didn't even know the taste of curry and he steadily refused to join us when invited to a meal in the orphanage or in a private home. This will sound shocking to modern ears but it was accepted as the norm in my early days. On the other hand, Herbert had come to India in the late thirties with a group of young people full of enthusiasm and new ideals. At home, they had belonged to the generation of those who had cast aside Victorian pomp and superficial dignity and the belief that the British were the superior,God-appointed bearers of the White Man's Burden. Kipling was out. The concept of Empire was now something to be ashamed of and while these young people, keenly evangelical, knew a loyalty that would not let them run to extremes, they were bound to have been influenced by such an atmosphere. In every generation we imbibe something of the theories and passionate feelings of our times.

So it was inevitable that there should be found a wide gap between them and the older missionaries who had spent a lifetime in a slower-moving world and who had been little affected even by the 1st World War when the shattering of worn-out notions had begun. It was a gap made up of differences in outlook and sentiment and even on scriptural interpretation which only love and the grace of God could bridge.

Between the two groups there were a few who had been out on the field since the late twenties and early thirties, long enough for India to have dulled a little the sharp edge of their enthusiasms and passionate opinions and to have given them some capacity for seeing the other person's point of view, at least, that is how I see myself, for I was one of that group. We were onlookers, helpless to do anything about the clash of opinions and ideals. It was not a comfortable position to be in. I had never wholly sympathised with the benevolent methods of the past generation of missionaries. I rarely had felt the desperate urge to better the physical lot of the Christian community. I was never moved to use my spare cash to dress the little girls around the compound in a manner more pleasing to my own tastes or to give some child a boarding school education. (I'm not necessarily proud of this attitude!) There was in me a streak of shrewdness that made me look through the act of charity to what it might do to the recipient or to others who might be thinking they had an equal right to my generosity. I still believe it to be the best plan to ask oneself before giving out money or goods: 'What is this going to do to this person?' It is a plan by which modern relief organisations function: grain for work and not charity. Employment is provided and relief grain paid out in wages each evening. Benefits are tremendous. Badly needed wells are dug, bad roads repaired and the people retain their dignity. While it is impossible to generalise or be dogmatic on this matter, it would seem that on our field at least, those who had had most lavished upon them emerged the least satisfactory.

Even so, I often found my heart aching for our older colleagues as, outvoted on most issues; they had to watch some work of a life-time swept away. Their grief was keenest when the issue at stake was the dismissal or retention of some unsatisfactory preacher. To the new generation, aflame with the desire to establish a self-supporting, self-governing, self-propagating church, the system of foreign-paid preachers presented the greatest stumbling block to the spread of the Gospel. Since many of these workers were living anything but exemplary Christian lives, some openly immoral, they had to go. The young people could not understand how such men had been allowed for so long to live on the Lord's money while dragging His name in the dust. The answer was, of course, that these men were still somebody's dearly loved boys, orphans snatched years ago from the streets or railway platforms, saved from starvation or from lives of unimaginable squalor. Brought up as Christians, they had been loved and prayed for, wept over and forgiven up to seventy times seven. This was something we (I include myself now with the younger ones) had not experienced. We had not yet admitted that in order to have the right to follow some of Paul's sterner principles of church discipline we must first know something of His suffering love for His converts, that we should not easily dismiss a man (which in our case meant sending him out to be exposed to further temptation) until we prayed over him with tears.

Undoubtedly there were workers who were totally unfitted for Christian service and who ought to have been put to other work long ago but as we ourselves grew older we came to see how easy it is to talk like this and how hard it must have been to carry out such a ruthless task. Living for years in the same compound with our present generation of orphans we also came to understand how such men could emerge from such a careful and loving upbringing. We watched our smiling and contented babies and toddlers, so endearing in their sun suits or the brightly coloured sweaters sent out from Britain, grow into bright-faced small schoolboys, affectionate, as obedient as most children, educated as far as their mentality allowed, nicely spoken and fairly good mannered, familiar with the Bible and knowing what sort of behaviour God expected of them, willing to go out in teams to evangelise the villages, able to take part in public prayer. Then, in adolescence, we watched them change. Those who had responded to the Gospel message, inviting the Lord Jesus Christ into their hearts and lives, grew into decent clean-living, healthy-minded Christians, in some cases becoming spiritual leaders. Those who had in their hearts resisted the Word, on whom the Holy Spirit had no influence, reverted to type before our eyes, coarsening, (becoming as their parents must have been) deceitful, immoral and in a few cases quite amoral. The latter type drifted away from us and was seen no more. But we had to face many times the problem of how to treat those who <u>did</u> return, some of them over and over again. Caught up in their own sinfulness; destitute, without work or home, these prodigals would come seeking help, for they had no one else to turn to. We could have sympathy then with our older colleagues who had succumbed, and given them work on the compound.

Now, beginning a new life in Tirbirwa after the intervening years of war, we were starting clean. There was not a paid Christian worker in the compound; the old preacher and Biblewoman had retired and moved away long before our arrival. We would now see whether or not the Christians would rise to their opportunities once their excuse was removed, that is, the delusion they had seemed to suffer from, that evangelism and Christian service was exclusively the task of the missionary and those whom he paid to help him.

While the Christians remained for some time polite but aloof we very quickly became acquainted with our non-Christian neighbours. We were near enough to them to hear their family quarrels over the hedge and to be disturbed when with flaming torches and frantic yells they attempted to drive from the village the evil spirits that had spoiled the crops or sent a disease among the cattle. Almost at once we were being asked to repair the damage done by the village 'doctor' who had rubbed black pepper into someone's eye or thrust a red hot needle into a child's abdomen to let out the evil spirit. We were asked to treat women suffering from their attempts to cure sterility by standing up to the neck in the river on a cold winter's night or by visits to an unscrupulous priest.

We had had no notion of setting up a dispensary for there was a Government hospital three miles away and some private practitioners in the town. But we soon learned that the hospital could not begin to cope with the teeming villages to the north, east and west of us, and the fees of private doctors were prohibitive to the poor. In vain we protested that we were not medically trained. Nothing would convince a villager that a Sahib could not lance an abscess, stitch up a broken head or remove a pea from a child's nose! We had come to live in the 'koti' the big house - and the 'koti' was part of their lives. They had always found help and succour there.

So one day, tired of treating an ever growing number on our back veranda, we turned out the old dispensary building. We would do as our predecessors had done; make ourselves available each Monday and Friday, these being market days in the town. Having whitewashed the walls inside and out and painted John 3:16 over the door in Hindi characters we were ready to begin. We inspected our stock of medicines and were dismayed. Bottles were mostly empty and the contents of packets had been eaten by white ants, all except a stock of Mag.Sulph. and another Magnesium something-or-other, the use of which escaped us. On one table stood three bottles of homeopathic tinctures, the three remedies which, before the advent of wonder drugs, were acknowledged as potent and effective in even the most unbelieving circles - the remedy for cholera, the cure for teething infants and that friend of all bumps and bruises - Arnica.

With our first scanty allowance from the Mission we bought Vaseline and sulphur powder, malaria pills, worm tablets and iodine (ours was a goitrous district) and these we set up on the men's side. In the women's room we put the homeopathic remedies left by Mrs Banks and a case of about forty tiny bottles of remedies which had been given to Herbert as part of his outfit and alongside them we placed a helpful looking book called *The Prescriber.* We had a feeling that with the increasing number of patients we should soon be driven by lack of money to use these remedies.

It was not lack of money, but our own ignorance that brought the wee pills into their own.

'I have parsota so badly; I can't sleep at night,' said the weary looking young mother. She had one baby in her arms and another clutching her sari. I longed to give her some release but what was parsota?

'Try the dictionary, Herbert called from the other room.'

I thumbed through the pages of the Hindi/English dictionary but could find no word like that. I called to the houseboy who was cleaning ears in the yard.

'What is parsota, Swarup?'

Swarup had been trained by Mary Follington to do some of the practical jobs in dispensary and he had a masterly way with eyes, ears and foreign bodies. He grinned and snuffled his feet.

'It is only among women; men don't have it.'

I decided it might be better not to ask him any more questions. I turned to the woman. 'Tell me just how you feel. What is that keeps you awake in the night?'

'Fires in my hands and my feet, and a fire here.' She touched the top of her head. 'And pains here —

I gazed round the dispensary in despair and bemoaned my ignorance. Would a dose of Mag. Sulph. do anything? or aspirin? or soda mints? I would have laughed, if it hadn't been so tragic. I tried to persuade her to go to the hospital but she simply went on shaking her head.

In despair I picked up the homeopathic book and searched through the symptoms. Burnings! Burnings everywhere and pains in small joints; pains that wander and that somehow have to do only with women. Cheers! Here it was. I turned to the case and found the indicated remedy. I made a poke of white paper and put in three days' medicine and also gave her pills for the teething infant.

She came back the following week bringing a neighbour. 'Please help her as you have helped me.' She had slept through the first night, for the baby too had been soothed and now the tooth was well through the gum.

A visit from Mr Vine eased our financial burden. Seeing the state of our shelves he arranged or us to have a small grant to restock the dispensary and have a small working balance. We charged one anna — equal to a farthing of our old money — and for that we could give three days' medicine. And because of the reasonable cost of the All India Missions Tablet Industry pills and the amazingly low cost of homeopathic remedies we were actually making a little on these medicines which helped to pay for the more expensive ointments.

We felt it wisest to make a charge, even from the poorest, having learned that the villager will never pour down the drain something he has paid for, however bitter it may taste. And to pay one's way preserves one's dignity. Those who came to us had walked far in the heat or the sun, but they had paid for their medicine; they hadn't begged. And if the anna scarcely covered the cost of the Vaseline in the ointment, they weren't to know that. Even the little one was made happy for the long trek home by the brightly coloured picture torn from an old Good Housekeeping magazine which we had not had the heart to spoil by slapping an anna worth of ointment on it!

Many of these villagers carried away with them something of the love of Christ — and His peace. Later on when the crowds thronging our compound had become more than we could manage, I would remember with nostalgia the days of this early ministry, the quiet talks with one group after another, for one had leisure to listen and to sympathise.

But the more we give of our sympathy in this loveless world, the more will people turn to us and the more costly the work becomes. The Lord was moved with compassion and healed those who came to Him, drawing bigger and bigger crowds until He was spent and weary. He could have escaped if He had wished to do so. And so can we escape involvement if we wish to. It is possible anywhere in the world to live one's Christian life, even among the sick and the poor, and to remain unscathed and unscarred; to give so much and no more.

There came a time, perhaps a year later, when I felt that I was giving too much and could not escape. There were as yet only three of us in the dispensary, ourselves and Swarup. I was having to interview every woman, first writing her name and village in the book, (Government regulations demanded this) and then onto her prescription paper, then listening to her trouble, deciding what she needed, measuring out the doses into bottle or poke, giving lucid instructions, taking her money and then moving her on. After dealing with a hundred or more, I was mentally exhausted. The problem was my hardness of hearing. I had a deaf-aid, one of the early models with earphones and a huge battery in a box as big as my Bible. It was simply in the way when I was working and, as is the manner of all deaf-aids, it magnified the 'noises off' which were many and strident.

Then one day the young Christian woman mentioned earlier appeared at my side. 'Memsahib, if I come and stand beside you during dispensary and repeat (in good Hindi!) what the women are saying to you, would it help?'

Would it help! I almost fell on her neck. 'You realise that we have no funds yet — we couldn't pay you an allowance?' I said, watching her anxiously.

'I know. That doesn't matter,' said Lillia. Another day she said: 'If you had someone sitting outside to write up the register and the prescription papers, you would only have to listen to symptoms and I could take over the actual dispensing.'

So her sister-in-law came to us and became clerk, selling Gospels and talking to patients as opportunity arose. Their two husbands who were home only at weekends offered to be responsible for preaching to the crowds gathered in the compound each Sunday. They had some talks recorded on tapes which our garden boy joyfully played to those waiting to be seen. This was something for which we had been praying. The Christians were now with us; we were working as a team. And it had been brought about by my affliction.

This was the first inkling I had had that my deafness was not simply a cross to be accepted, to be borne by the grace of God with as much grace as possible. It was something God could use in His purposes, in this case in answering our own prayers. How many feelings of frustration I could have saved myself; how many moments of despicable self-pity; had I seen this before, that offered up to Him to be used as He willed, for my good and for the good of others, this affliction could be one of the greatest blessings of my life. To learn to live with it could mean much more than a sudden, miraculous healing would have meant.

I have written this, not to decry miracles of healing; I would never do that; but that my words might comfort or challenge those who have prayed for healing, perhaps with tears and certainly with faith, and nothing has happened. The Lord knows which will lead to our ultimate good or, more important, to the fulfilling of some purpose of His own — the sudden miracle or the miracle of sustaining grace, triumphant grace. If we are right in interpreting Paul's 'thorn in the flesh' as a physical disability which the Lord refused to remove, then we with a permanent handicap are in good company! And the same grace promised to Paul is available to us; Romans 8:28 still holds good. God is making all things work together for good to those who love Him, to the called according to His purposes. How much poorer in personality many of us would be if we had never been faced with and triumphed over the temptation to feel sorry for ourselves, had we never been able to prove that God does give songs in the night.

Before long I was to see another reason why I had not been healed.

CHAPTER TWELVE

Adventure in the New India

While we were getting to know our new neighbours, events were moving fast in India. Independence had come at last and with it some of the usual attendant dangers and evils. The worst of the trouble was over by the time we returned from furlough. The antagonism between Muslims and Hindus over Partition had settled itself in our district and the two communities seemed to be shaking down together. Many of the Muslim families had, of course, fled to Pakistan.

In our remote village we scarcely noticed the changes that Independence had already brought until we needed to travel by train. Then we saw changes both bad and good. The railways had been nationalised. Notices appeared in the compartments - This is your railway; it belongs to you. Take care of it. Many travellers gleefully ignored the second half and took the first part literally. Light bulbs disappeared; electric fittings were wrenched from their sockets; mirrors and hooks disappeared from the toilets and the American cloth covering the seats in the upper-class compartments was ripped off, leaving exposed the springs in their bed of cotton wool.

To make matters worse, the rural population who, up to now, had walked everywhere or jogged along in bullock-carts now realized that they had as much right as anybody else to use the trains. If they had no money for a ticket, well, that was a minor detail, especially if they were on pilgrimage to some holy bathing place. Village youths studying in the nearby city school or college, who in the past had risen with the dawn and, carrying precious shoes under their arms, had walked the long miles each morning and evening now boarded the trains without tickets, boarded in such numbers that ticket collectors and guards stood helplessly by. These lads had a preference for the upper-class compartments. They filled the upper berths and if no other space was available they sat on the window sills, their knees poking into the backs of seated passengers and their bodies completely blocking any passage of air. Perhaps this situation was more pronounced on our line which ran through N. Bihar, one of the most densely populated rural areas in the world.

It was during this period that I had a most frightening experience. I had to meet our daughter, then about eight years old, who was coming home for the winter holidays from school in Darjeeling. She would be travelling part of the way with the school party bound for Calcutta and I was to pick her up at Parbatipur where our local line and the Calcutta line parted company. Having arranged to visit a friend who lived near this town I left a day earlier than would have been necessary, which was fortunate in the light of what happened to me.

I spent the first night in a women's compartment, packed to suffocation. Women pressed on me from both sides, they filled the upper berths and crouched on the floor in a packed mass making movement impossible, and some intrepid spirits sat in the open window sills. I actually saw by the bright light of the festival moon one of these girls lean backward and receive a kiss from a man leaning from the next compartment! I would have thought this impossible in India had I not seen it with my own eyes.

Early next morning we arrived at Katihar which was the end of the Indian line. Here I had to board a train which would take me across the strip of newly-formed Pakistan which had virtually cut Darjeeling off from the rest of N. India. A new link line was under construction which would eventually bypass Pakistan and run straight through to Assam but it was not yet open.

The station here was milling with people, mostly pilgrims. I ensconced myself in the dining room, my bedding-roll at my feet, for the waiting room was filthy beyond description, My train came in during the morning but I found that I couldn't get near it, let alone board it. I watched it steam away, the yelling, frustrated crowd almost sweeping me off my feet, and returned to the dining room. Three more trains came in during the day and each time I was swept from the doors. By nightfall I was frightened. What would happen to June if I didn't arrive in time to pick her up? Would the escorts leave her at the station hoping that I would turn up, or would they take her on to Calcutta? In either case she would be terrified; she had always had a dread of being left alone on an Indian railway platform. I began to beseech the Lord piteously to help me.

When the night train was due, the waiter took pity on me. 'Come, Memsahib,' he said, picking up my bedding roll, 'I'll see if I can get you into the soda-walla's compartment.' The vender of soft drinks had his own cubby hole in every train in those days. I agreed thankfully though I knew somewhere beneath the numbness that this was going to mean a passing of money — whether it meant a tip or a bribe I was too tired to work out — which appalled me when I thought of it later. One thing this experience did for me was to make me more compassionate than I had ever been toward poor people who were caught stealing — and they were legion. None of us knows just what we might be tempted to do if our children were starving or were in sudden danger. When I think of the way I used my elbows, for instance, as I pushed my way through these crowds, people I had come to serve, I feel hot with shame.

The waiter was doing the elbowing now as I followed him, clinging to his dirty white coat. Then I saw a huge Pathan standing just inside the door of a third class compartment. He had his arms stretched out before him, his hands against the wall and his body curved to make space at his feet where his wife was crouched.

'Can I come in there with your wife?' I asked him, holding the waiter back. He nodded. My bedding roll was thrust in somehow and I joined the little lady on the floor, managing to find a generous tip for the waiter who had been so kind.

At Parbatipur coolies pulled me out, stiff and sore and incredibly dirty. It was the morning of the third day. I was in good time, having forgotten about the visit to my friend. The school party wouldn't be leaving Stiliguri at the foot of the Darjeeling hills until late afternoon and would arrive here during the night. There was ample time for me to have a wash, to eat, and to sleep if I could find a bench on which to stretch myself! I saw the train from Calcutta standing on the opposite platform, ready to leave for Stiliguri and it was half empty. Why not? I thought as a suggestion struck me. I could be in Stiliguri before the school party arrived, and there I would find civilized amenities.

'Get me into that train,' I said to a coolie.

'It's just going, Memsahib,' he said. 'Run!'

He picked up my bedding roll and flung it into a first-class compartment. I stumbled after it and fell at the feet of two British planters who were still in pyjamas. I started to tell them what had happened and as I spoke one went to the door as the train moved and grabbed a tray of tea from a passing waiter. I had a shower, ate my breakfast, and then was helped up to an upper berth where I slept until we reached Stiliguri.

With what relief and thankfulness I watched the school train coming slowly down that fabulous Darjeeling mountain railway, naughty schoolboys standing on the running board even when they seemed to be hanging over a precipice.

June was thrilled and excited to see me sooner than expected. We hugged each other and laughed, and my tiredness disappeared because I believed that my troubles were over. But they were not, when the coolie dumped June's trunk on the floor of the waiting room the lid flew open from the back. Both hinges were broken. I looked at it in dismay.

'We can't take it like that,' I said, remembering the jostling crowds and packed compartments which were still to be faced. 'But we'll go and have some tea before we worry about it.'

The dining room was almost empty, the school children not yet mustered for tea. June led me to a table away from the door and in her usual friendly fashion was soon in conversation with a British planter seated at the next table. I wasn't taking much notice. I was picturing in my mind all that could happen to that trunk. I saw it knocked from the coolie's head as he wrestled with the crowd, its contents spilling just where it would be impossible to pick them up.

'Why are you crying?' I heard my daughter say. I looked up, ready to apologise, but the man was smiling at her.

'Because I have a little girl like you at home in England and I haven't seen her for two years.'

June looked shocked. 'Why doesn't she live with you here?'

His smile faded. 'Her Mummy doesn't like India. She prefers to live in England.'

'Poor man' said June. 'I guess you're lonely.'

'That's enough, June,' I said. "Drink up your tea.'

She looked at me. 'Mummy's worried about my trunk,' she said confidingly to the man. 'It's broke!'

He looked at me enquiringly. 'It's the hinges,' I said. 'Both broken; I can't take it as it is on that awful journey.' I told him something of the difficulties I had had on the way here. 'I'm thinking of risking the new link line. They tell me here that it is open as far as Katihar.'

He leaned forward, looking dismayed. 'But you mustn't. Nobody knows what the conditions are. There will be no amenities as yet. If the train broke down, or something worse, you would have nowhere to go; none to help you.'

'The conditions couldn't be worse than they were crossing East Pakistan,' I said.

'Yes, they could. They could be infinitely worse. You must go back the way you came. Please. Don't worry about the trunk. All it needs is a bit of rope. I'll send my man to the bazaar now to get some. Excuse me a moment.'

When he returned, June had left me to join her friends who were pouring into the dining room. He came and sat in her place, pushed her cup to one side and put his elbows on the table.

'Why do you do it?' he said.

'Do what?

'Why do you stay in this uncomfortable country? It's obvious that you're not doing it to make money as I am.'

I pushed my hair back from my face, damp as it was with sweat and dirt. He had undoubtedly noted my cheap frock and my scuffed Bata sandals. He was probably the sort of person who thinks all missionaries are fools and fanatics, wasting their time. I looked at him and didn't speak.

He smiled. 'Tell me,' he said. 'I really do want to know.'

There was not a shade of derision on his face as I spoke of the tremendous power of the call of God in the heart, a call of God cannot be ignored. I spoke of the peace of mind, no matter how great the difficulties, of knowing one is in the will of God, caught up in His plan for the world, of knowing that everything is in His hands, that like the Israelites of old one is being fed by the integrity of His heart and guided by the skilfulness of His hands, not by one's own.

'H-mm! Out of the rat-race, the eternal worry about money. Is that what you mean? But what do you do out here?'

I told him something about the dispensary, the church and the preaching of the Gospel.

'But what do you tell them? Pretend I'm a Hindu and preach to me.'

He was giving me an opportunity and I took it. We talked for almost an hour and I forgot all my troubles in the joy of discussing the great fundamentals of our faith, the reality of redemption through the cross of Christ and the power of the Resurrection with an intelligent, keen-minded, but nominal Christian. I never heard what effect the discussion had on him but the encounter made the journey meaningful to me. As did another encounter with a Muslim this time, as the train thundered through Pakistan.

We had found the station at Parbatipur as thronged as had been the platform at Katihari only now the pilgrims were on their way home. The same agitated people rushed to and fro, shouting and stumbling over baggage and children. June and I stood still and I prayed while the coolie, the trunk on his head, urged us from behind to move and look for a place. Instead there came to us an answer to our prayer. A bearer in imposing livery came up and said his master would make room for us in his compartment. The master was a high court judge on transfer with his goods and his three wives and he had a reserved compartment for himself. He was interested in Christianity and opened up the subject as soon as we were settled. So while June slept beside me and the three wives giggled behind their purdah and finally slept we talked about the Lord. It was evident that this wasn't the first time he had been moved by the truth of the Gospel. He was so earnest, so perturbed by the implication of it that one could almost hear him thinking: "Almost thou persuadest me to be a Christian." But he didn't say it. He would know too well the terrible cost of such an admission to a man in his position. I never saw him again.

By the time June and I boarded the train for our final twenty-five miles, the festival period was over. We sat in solitary comfort, and never had the flat uninspiring landscape seemed so beautiful. As the years passed the conditions on the railway did not improve. Boarding passengers surged to the doors as soon as the trains drew in, preventing alighting passengers from getting out; youths travelled on the running-boards or squatted on the roofs in spite of the many that had been swept off as trains entered a tunnel. But the situation eased a little when it became possible to book sleeping berths on all long distance journeys even in the third class. And we were now third-class passengers. The upper-class compartments were taken over by the new aristocracy — merchants, lawyers, judges, military officers and railway staff travelling on a pass. The Europeans — missionaries, tourists and hippies — moved into the third class where huge compartments had been turned into sleeping accommodation. These compartments are rather like the bogies of a corridor train. A narrow passage runs down one side and opening into it are cubicles, about sixteen in number, not enclosed by doors but completely open to view. Each cubicle has six berths, three on each side, the middle berth dropping down in the daytime to form a backrest for the lower seat. So all the occupants must go to bed and rise at the same time which could be unpleasant at times. But there was a guard at each door and only berth holders were allowed to enter which ensured a measure of peace and a feeling of safety.

Suffer Little Children

During the early days of our time in Tirbirwa, before the clamouring crowds overtook us taking up all our time, I was able to continue the two meetings for village children begun by Mary. The best time of the day to catch these children was just after dawn. Once the sun was up they would be away, leading the goats or the cattle to pasture.

One morning I made for Bhitbirwa, a village about half a mile away and from which our cook came daily. It was the rainy season. As I crossed the stretch of common land behind our house, the high cirrus cloud suddenly caught the first flash of the yet un-risen sun and the sky was filled with tiny pink feathers and every puddle shone like opal. The green corn was breast high, hiding the village from view, but as I began to walk along one of the raised paths that divided field from field two small boys who had been watching for me raced to meet me. Shivpujan (worshipper of Shiv) took the flannel-graph board and my bag of books while Bandhu (friend) took the brass elephant bell from me and raced ahead, ringing it vigorously and shouting; 'Yesu Masih – Jesus Christ has come!' Out of the alleyways the children came tumbling, most of them naked save for a bit of rag around their middles.

An old woman, skinny and wrinkled, the rents in her dirty sari tied together in knots, but with surprisingly bright intelligent eyes, walked alongside me.

'What are you teaching our children?' she said.

'I'm teaching them that God loves them,' I replied. 'Do you object?'

She waved a hand in a gesture of contempt. 'What's the good of that?' she said. 'If your God is a God of love, He won't do them any harm. You should teach them how to ward off the evil ones.'

'If your children come to trust Yesu, no evil will be able to touch them. Come along and listen today.'

I set up the flannel-graph board on our cook's family threshing floor and the children sat cross-legged on the ground. My two self-appointed monitors (the only two wearing dhoti and shirt) took their stand behind the group, long bamboo canes in their hands by which they could tap the heads of squirming infants on the front row if they grew too restless. The lesson that day was on the lost sheep. After some noisy, un-tuneful singing of appropriate choruses I put the Good Shepherd on the board, His sheep behind Him.

'That's not right' interrupted the old woman. 'Our shepherds go behind and drive the sheep – with a stick.'

'But this is the Good Shepherd. He doesn't drive – He leads. The sheep, who love Him, follow Him.'

But here was one sheep who didn't follow; who thought the grass was greener on the other side. He had a wonderful time of it while daylight lasted, doing just what he liked, but when sudden darkness fell, with the baying of approaching wolves, he found himself alone and was terrified. He fled, tearing himself on thorns and stumbling over stones, falling forward into a pit. Then, lying helpless, with the wolf waiting for him at the rim of the pit, he remembered the shepherd and began to cry. And now here comes the shepherd, out looking for him with lantern and stave. First he fights with the wolf and kills him, then, torn and bleeding he lifts the sheep from the pit. A drawn-out 'ah-a-a' of satisfaction escapes from the children as the shepherd appears, carrying the sheep across his shoulder.

An explanation followed – it must follow, for these children would not automatically think of Jesus as would Western children. I looked at the old woman. Her eyes were suspiciously bright as she stared back at me, and she threw up her hands in a strange gesture of despair. Then she said: 'Jesus Masih is for you. We have our own gods,' and drawing her sari over her face she walked away.

It was a long time before I saw her again though I had heard that she had tried to dissuade Shivpujan and Bandhu from attending the meetings. Then one day in February of the following year she again gave me something to think about. Leaving the village after the class, the usual trail of children behind me, I became aware of my two monitors shushing the chattering group of smaller children. I couldn't tell why they were whispering but looking round I saw the object of their interest. I went closer. It was a little girl lying on a filthy bed and she was literally skin and bones, with hollow eyes and parched lips.

We were not as familiar then as we are now with pictures of starving Asian children but there was no mistaking this case. The child was dying of starvation. I was puzzled, for the children of the village were looking better after the winter when food was more plentiful. On our northern plains the 'hungry months' end with September when the sweet corn is harvested. Then the herd boys go out with the animals, gnawing at a corn cob roasted black in the fire, and through the winter most of them can reckon on one meal of rice or chapattis on their return.

My children deserted me when the mother came out looking sullen and a little frightened. All I could learn from her was that the child had been ill. No, she had not had any medicine. I remonstrated with her, reminding her that our dispensary was just across two fields and that we never refused medicine to those who were too poor to pay. In the end she promised to send her son after me to get medicine. I felt I could at least send some powdered milk and glucose.

Walking away, I wondered what the mystery could be that my two boys had not wanted me to know, when I became aware of the old woman walking beside me.

'He won't come,' she said.

'Who won't come?'

'The boy for the medicine. The girl is *charwaha*.' A *charwaha* (the word is translated 'Corban' in Mark 7:11) is an offering made in sacrifice. At the festival of 'Chat' the special day when the women gather at the nearest river and make offerings to the goddess Kali, this widow woman had had nothing to offer. It had occurred to no one to give her something to offer, thus allaying her fears, so, terrified that Kali would take revenge by inflicting some evil on the son, she had given her little girl who was ill anyway. She had not made an open sacrifice – that would have brought the police on her, but by withholding food and drink was starving the child to death.

The old woman looked at my stricken face. 'Your Yesu Masih wouldn't demand that?' she asked.

'No! Never, never!' I said passionately. 'Yesu Masih loves little children.' We walked in silence for a little while then I stopped and looked her in the face. 'But He was very hard on those who drove little children from Him, who prevented them from coming to Him and believing in Him. He said it would be better for them if a millstone were hung around their necks and they were cast into the sea.'

CHAPTER FOURTEEN

A New Service

'Come and look here!'

We had gathered on the flat roof of the Yunas' house for the Sunday hymn-singing and family prayers, for the evening had turned muggy and airless. The meeting over, Sudhan had risen and was standing looking out over the fields. We joined him and caught our breath in dismay. Like a huge grey snake gliding through the green of the monsoon landscape people were moving toward our compound.

'The evening train has come in' said Sudhan. 'These people are coming for tomorrow's dispensary.'

We turned and looked northward toward the Deear. From that direction and from the east they were coming, crossing fields in single file, bundles on heads, toddlers on shoulders, babies on hips. They too were grey streaks on the green for this was no holiday crowd in gaily dyed garments on their way to the Mela (Religious Fair), but desperately poor people coming to us for help, clad in the off-white garb of the Bihar villagers of those days. The peace of our Sunday was shattered.

'But what are we going to do?' I cried. 'We can't treat all these folk!'

'There's only one thing for it,' said Sudhan. 'You'll have to open every day, not only on market days.'

'But if we do that,' Lillia objected, 'how will we get the medicines made up? There are only five of us.'

'If you open every day you won't need to work till evening. You could close firmly at 12.30 and use the afternoon to make the medicines and tidy up.'

'It would be the end of our outside evangelistic work,' said Herbert. 'There would be no more days at the Mela.'

'Melas?' Sudhan cried. 'You won't need to go to the Melas; the Melas are coming to you.'

It was true. We must have treated seven hundred people that day and our cook insisted that as many had gone away. This was something we were going to have to face, as long as we remained in Tirbirwa we would be pressed with crowds. The only alternative to attending to them was to pack up and go away.

The problems were enormous. We had to try to make sure that people were being served in the order in which they had come; that the old and weak were not being pushed to the rear over and over again. We issued tickets, fifty each of red, white, blue, green and yellow, half to the men and half to the women. And though it was often a strain to keep to the colours as we were harassed by importunate, yelling, ticketless people outside or by arrogant, better-class neighbours who took advantage of their position and their friendship with us to get priority treatment; we persevered and slowly the people learned that it was useless to jump the white queue if one had a red ticket. One might as well sit and be quiet.

We were also convinced that we must never lose sight of every part of our commission - to preach, to teach, and to heal. The Lord, as pressed by crowds as we were, had never allowed the healing ministry to crowd out His preaching, His teaching and training of His disciples or His quiet times with His Father. Neither must we allow the crowds to hinder our preaching, our care for the spiritual growth of the church, the preservation of our own spiritual equilibrium.

We now opened daily, beginning at 7.30am with prayers in the church. Over at the dispensary, copies of the booklet *The Day of Salvation* were handed out to those who had no tickets and who would have to wait over to the next day. These tracts, well read by those who could read (and they all read aloud) would be exchanged for a ticket when, after lunch, Herbert returned to preach to a new crowd and to sell Gospels. The folk listened well and bought the Gospels gladly, no doubt thinking that all this was part of the 'magic' of their cure. But those Gospels were going out into every part of the district and we trusted that they would be read aloud by the bright boy of the family when they gathered round the fire in the village square on winter nights and that someone would understand and accept the truth.

Nothing before, or since those hectic days has offered to those of us who worked in the dispensary such opportunity to test the grace of God offered to us all in times of need. We were tried in varying degrees, of course, according to our temperaments. Indians, for instance, are not easily flapped; they tend not to expend themselves emotionally as we do (often needlessly). The clamouring, yelling, suffering people, from whom all the proverbial patience of the East had fled, did not harass our helpers as they did us.

Especially me! Humanly speaking, I was least fitted for a service so full of strain. Not long-suffering or gentle by nature, I was particularly exasperated by stupidity. Fortified by a good quiet time, reminded of the Lord's presence by small texts I had pinned up around my window, I would be fine until around eleven o'clock. After that I would begin to feel myself slipping. So many more women to see and every one so reluctant to move on.

'Did you say my husband was to take these pills with water?'

I was concentrating on an old woman who seemed to have a pain in the nape of her neck. I turned with a sigh to the wife of the malaria patient who had returned to the window. 'Yes, plenty of water.'

'Hot or cold?'

'It doesn't matter. Give him plenty.'

I focused again on the pain in the neck. The old woman was toothless and mumbled her words. She seemed to have pins and needles in her hands and feet - 'jhin-jhin' she called it, which I thought most expressive. It could be malnutrition, but what to give her?

'Did you say he was to take three pills a day?'

I felt myself beginning to glare at the woman. (Oh, Lord. Let my words be with grace.) 'Look, sister, he takes three pills a day with plenty of water. And don't worry; he will get better. Tell him we give them in the Name of Yesu Masih.'

The old woman dealt with, I turned to a young girl holding a baby covered in sores from head to foot. The skin had peeled from the soles of its feet.

'How long has the child been like this?' I asked, gazing at it in horror. She shrugged. 'Three months,' she said simply. Having received her pills and some ointment in a small earthen pot she was given a push by her more alert neighbour who then pointed to her own child. It had diarrhoea. 'He has a cold too, hasn't he?' I said, eyeing the dirty nose where half a dozen flies had settled. She looked at him, and she too shrugged. Then she cleaned the child's nose with thumb and forefinger and wiped it on the side of the window, her immediate neighbour obligingly making way for her to do so!

I now turned to a group of giggling girls whom I had bypassed because I couldn't get a sensible answer out of them. They were still giggling and each question brought the sari over their smiling mouths. I felt my patience cracking and prayed for grace. Then a woman behind them, who was not hampered by an urge to speak with grace, opened her mind. She was a strong-faced woman who probably had a dozen such giggling daughters-in-law at home. Her words were blistering. The giggling ceased. Symptoms were described, strong teeth dragged at the knots in the sari where the coins were secreted and within a few minutes they were gone.

My deliverer was not so easy. 'I have hunger,' she said, 'but when my meal is set before me my throat says: "I will not swallow" and my stomach says: "I will not take it."'

I stared at her in astonishment as she stood tenderly stroking her bare stomach. She looked at me with some exasperation.

'I have great hunger in my stomach. That's what I mean.'

The homeo book came to my rescue. There it was in black and white. Hunger disappears at sight of food.

Just before noon, there was a new tumult outside. 'Somebody has fainted in the queue,' said Lillia. The 'queue' was a bamboo barrier which we had fixed up to ensure a modicum of quiet in the immediate vicinity of the building. It was about ten foot long and just wide enough for one person. The men tended to keep to single file in their queue but the women packed themselves in so tightly that, once in, it was impossible to get out. I could see the woman, her face bloodless, her head sagging, but she was kept upright by the press. Now I am prone to faints and I know the agony one endures when coming round from a faint if one is prevented from lying down — often by well-meaning people! I shouted to the women behind her to come out of the barrier so that I could get her out, but they had waited a long time for these places and they had no intention of giving them up.

There is a silent obstinacy in many village women which is often their only weapon of defence in a man's world, and it can be maddening. Here it was at its worst. I was suddenly blazing with anger. I began to pull them out one by one, grabbing whichever portion of their clothes or anatomy came to hand. I got the woman stretched on the ground; someone brought water which she refused to touch when she came round, it being the Muslim fast of Ramadan and she must not even sip water until after sunset! Deflated and ashamed, I tried to excuse my anger by lecturing the women on being thoughtful for others in their suffering. But I knew that, according to their ideals, my display of righteous anger had been more sinful than their indifference. It was something they did not understand.

I returned to my window, shaken and trembling, but managed to finish the morning's work. Once in my room, however, I sat alone and wept, wept for my miserable failure before the Christians and the villagers. This was not the first time I had wept. There had been other defeats if not so spectacular and appalling.

I had long since ceased to blame my handicap for my defeats yet there was an underlying fear that because of it I would never come to absolute victory over my impatient spirit. Now, mingled with my shame was the fear that I might become so deaf that I would be useless for any sort of missionary work and so put an end to this service for both of us. My evening work, for instance, was already becoming impossible. I had been in the habit of slipping out when my household chores were finished to spend an hour with the people camping in the compounds waiting for next day's dispensary. I would join them as they squatted around the small fires they had lit between two bricks on which to cook their rice, and would try to make up for the lack of personal contact during the day. I would encourage them to talk about themselves and their troubles. Then lead onto God's love for them and his provision in Christ. But this also was becoming too much of a strain. I could speak to them but I couldn't hear what they said to me. I might be nodding assent when they had said something outrageous or made some erroneous statement or I might smile when they were relating some tragedy.

The deaf aid? This became less and less of an aid as I became more mentally tired, as any deaf person will understand. The aid magnifies sound which is a tremendous help, but along with hardness of hearing there is in most cases an accompanying slowing up of perception, of comprehension. The meaning of sounds penetrates more slowly into the brain. A person speaks and the voice is loud enough, maybe too loud, but the words mean nothing. A lowering of vitality can increase the dullness - a cold in the head, mental exhaustion or just plain tiredness. This is something many people don't understand so they become impatient with a relative who seems to hear so well at one time and become completely and stupidly deaf at another.

On this unhappy day I beseeched the Lord to show me something that I could do without using my ears, a service that would be just as important and meaningful as had been my evangelism or my healing of the sick.

After a while I lay down for a short rest and opened the magazine of the Evangelical Fellowship of India (EFI) which had come that morning. The first thing I saw was an announcement of a competition for Christian writers. The Committee of the literature arm of the EFI were feeling a need for something different in the way of Christian literature, books that would attract the man in the street, ordinary people who were not interested in our theological or devotional literature. A Christian novel — or story if you shy at the word 'novel' — might answer this need. Writers were invited to submit stories demonstrating Christianity in action. The winning effort would be published in English first for the All India Book Club and then in all the regional languages.

This, I thought, was for me. I believed that the Lord had directed me to the notice in answer to my desperate prayer. Not that I considered myself a writer. I had attempted a story for the young people of the Mission, and Sown in the Dust was already on the Mission's bookstalls. But the possibility of reaching the people in India by writing had not occurred to me.

Written during the long evenings when Herbert was shut away in the office, my effort won first prize. Like all fiction it contained a good deal of truth. The story was set among the Christians of Calcutta; we had lived there for three months while Herbert supplied for the pastor of a Baptist church. A young Indian Christian had addressed our final Christian Endeavour group, giving his personal testimony. He had just resigned from one of the well-known travel agencies as a protest against bribery and corruption in the firm. He told our young people that he had no idea as to where he would find another job but he was confident that God would take care of him, he quoted the text: "For promotion cometh neither from the east nor from the west... God is the judge: He putteth down one and setteth up another." (1Cor.9:22)

I called my book *Promotion* and showed the struggles of a young Christian when his ambitions began to clash with his desire to be the best for God. It was kindly received by many, Christians and non-Christians, though some missionaries retained their mistrust of the novel as a medium of the Gospel. Some of my friends thought I was wasting my time as I went on with this form of writing — I sensed this more by their silence than their comments! I shall always remember with gratitude those who encouraged me to go on, particularly Patricia Strong and Irene Stephens.

There came a day when I too began to wonder if I might not be writing something better and deeper. Perhaps I could produce a book that would be acclaimed by all the evangelical elite of India if not of the world! These aspirations were cut short by Paul's words to the Corinthians: "To the weak became I as weak, that I might gain the weak. I am made all things to all men that I might by all means save some." If Paul with his mighty intellect could so forget the plaudits of men as to become weak with the weak because it was necessary that the weak (intellectually and spiritually weak, we presume) should understand the Gospel, then I too with no such mighty intellect could afford to bring myself to the level of the poorly educated or not very intelligent, to the man in the street, the giddy young among the Christians, or the children. By means of stories revealing the Christian life, the way Christians react to trouble and sorrow, the way they bring up their children and above all, making clear the way of salvation in Christ through faith alone, perhaps I could 'save some' or help some young people to a deeper life of faith.

So the books went out and the Lord blessed them and used them and multiplied them. They were translated into every regional language of India and then were used further afield, in Pakistan, Thailand, and Hong Kong. They found their way into bookshops in South Africa, and Nigeria. I felt as the small boy must have felt who gave his poor supper to the Lord and saw it multiplied to feed five thousand.

Lillia and our other helpers, thrilled to have some part in this exciting ministry freed me from all dispensary duties after midday so I was able eventually to make some regular contribution to Christian magazines — to the Light of Life magazine and, in its beginnings, the organ of the Fellowship of Evangelical Students. Later I was invited to help prepare a series of graded Sunday School lessons. This was an ambitious programme begun by the Christian Education arm of EFI the aim being to publish them in every major language of India. We used an American series and my part was to help with the adapting of them for use in India, simplifying and shortening them, cutting out all American illustrations and replacing them with stories of Indian life. It was a most interesting and satisfactory task, for thanks to the zeal and indefatigable efforts of Anna Nixon who first had the vision, and to Missions, including our own, who helped financially, this tremendous vision became reality. Today the Sunday School manuals, in English and in all the major languages, are being used by the ever-growing number of nationals engaged in the teaching of children.

So I learned afresh one of the most precious lessons God has to teach us, namely, that there is meaning and purpose in every disappointment, every frustration of plans, every problem and every grief allowed by Him to visit those who love Him, those who are called according to His purpose. It was during the hours of silence and loneliness that I learned the craft which transformed my missionary service, giving me a sense of fulfilment I hadn't known before. When I remember how I fretted during the early days of my deafness and also how nearly we both came to refusing to be banished again to the lonelier side of the province, I am thankful to the Lord who laid His hand upon our hot hearts and brought acquiescence and peace.

Perhaps it is true, as someone has suggested, that God's reason for sending some of us abroad is not only that we might make His name known and spread the good news of salvation in Christ but that He might do something in us which He could not do in our sheltered home environment. If our prayers are that He will make of us all that He wants us to be are true and sincere then, if we are willing, He will place us in the situation where our prayers can be answered - at any cost.

I can't say that at the end of our seventeen years in Tirbirwa my prayers for myself were wholly and finally answered. My prayer had always been that, under provocation, I might become more patient and gentle with the stupid and the ignorant. When we were facing the final weeks of our service in the dispensary, I prayed that they might be, just for once, completely victorious with not one impatient word or gesture. Yet more than once I had to say ruefully: 'Missed it again.'

Perhaps we all have to face up to this problem of the 'sin that so easily besets us', these humiliating faults that cause us to go on suffering defeat no matter how earnestly we have asked God to remove them. They are part of our make-up and they seem to keep alongside us all of our pilgrim way, skulking behind the hedge, keeping up with us, ready to pounce and fell us to the ground. Perhaps they serve to teach us that God has no instant perfection to hand out to us. It wouldn't be good for us if He had, as He told the Israelites that he would not remove their enemies at once but little by little; "lest the beasts of the field increase upon thee". If God were to work some miracle so that from the word 'Go' we would never again lose our temper, or lose control over our gossipy tongues, or exaggerate, or even lie, we might find that the wild beasts of pride and self-righteousness have us in their grip making us contemptuous of others' weaknesses, critical, cold and entirely unusable in His hands. These odd 'thorns' which He never seems to deal with, always the humiliating ones, keep us walking humbly with our God, relying on him for continued grace, not trusting our own strength.

I am not competent to say what Herbert learned during these difficult seventeen years. Patience under provocation and tenderness toward the sick and the weak were not the virtues he lacked. The clamouring, importunate crowds didn't upset him as they did me. He talked to the ignorant villagers as to brothers and they loved him. Indeed one could say with truth that some of them almost worshipped him. There was the woman who came for medicine for a sick husband and came three times and failed to get a ticket. We knew nothing about her until we heard with horror that in desperation her husband had told her to take up some of the dust Herbert had walked on and bring it home. She had done so; the man had eaten it and recovered!

As I have said before, the years in Tirbirwa were lonely ones. We were cut off from the rest of our colleagues, meeting them only at Conference time. We didn't feel this so much while the children were small and still with us, not even as they became old enough to go to boarding school. We were able to have three glorious weeks with them during the summer in Ootacamund and then came the joy of welcoming them home for the Christmas holidays, of seeing them so well in health and hearing their happy tales of school life. But in 1957 we had to leave them at home in Ireland. June was seventeen and had passed her final examination – the Senior Cambridge; we left her in the Royal Victoria Hospital for nursing training. Michael was not yet fifteen, a vulnerable age and not the easiest time to face such a parting but if we had taken him back with us he would have had to return after two years, and alone. He had been attending Herbert's old school for a year so we felt that the wisest plan was to leave him there in boarding among boys he had come to know. But Tirbirwa without the children seemed a bleak prospect as we faced it again.

The factor which contributed most to our burden during the years we spent there was our helplessness in the face of grievous tragedies that we were unable to avert or appease. There were the sick people who stood daily outside our dispensary beseeching us to help them but whom we could not begin to treat. I believe they brought more weariness to our minds and bodies than the huge crowds we were able to deal with. Then there were the hungry we couldn't feed for they were around us on every side in their hundreds. Only in times of dire famine could we help them when Herbert was given charge of three or four villages to give out the Government rations. Even then we were continually harassed by villagers begging him to take over their villages for only then, they said, would the grain go where it was needed and not into the granaries of the rich.

Thirdly, there were the sicknesses and the deaths we were powerless to prevent because the sufferers were denied our medicine, the victims of smallpox, for instance, or those who had been declared not ill but possessed with a demon which must not be tampered with. And once, at least, in a case of human sacrifice.

Yet we had made our district ring with the name of Christ. Hundreds, if not thousands came to associate the Name of Jesus with healing, love and peace.

'Say that Name for me again,' an old, old woman cried to Herbert, squatting in the dust outside his office. 'No, I'm not going to the dispensary. I don't need medicine; I'm better. I just want to hear again that Name that gave me such peace here,' and she laid a hand on her bony chest.

Then there was the middle-aged woman whom I found wandering round our garden long after she had received her medicine. She was the mother of a lad who had been tragically murdered. 'Why are you still here?' I asked her gently. She smiled at me and said: 'Let me stay awhile. There is peace here.'

All over our district the medicine was called Jesus Christ's medicine. People chose it in defiance of the Babaji (the Indian equivalent of the witch doctor) and often suffered persecution for their choice. Sometimes the choice marked a crisis. A Brahmin came from a far distant village one evening, appearing on our veranda for he was a personal friend. Herbert had stayed in his home with Ernest Oliver, years before, when they were on an evangelistic tour. They had loved him, finding him humble and lovable. He had been prepared to risk breaking his caste in order to give them hospitality. Now he was in great distress. His little son was dying and the local doctors had not been able to do anything for him. Herbert left him in the garden while he went to the dispensary to get the medicine he felt the child needed and when he returned the man was picking leaves from our Asoka tree, a tree sacred to the Hindus.

'What are you going to do with those?' Herbert asked him.

'I'm going to offer them up for the life of my son,' he replied, but he was going to offer them to the goddess Kali.

'Brother, we give you this medicine in the Name of the Lord Jesus Christ,' Herbert said gently. 'Are you going to trust Jesus Masih, or these?' and he flicked the leaves with his finger.

The man gazed at him and there was agony in his eyes, the agony of decision. Then he said: 'I'll trust Jesus Masih,' and threw the leaves on the ground.

In spite of all his care for the sick, the constant preaching of the Gospel, the many personal talks, there was a disappointing lack of response. Thousands of Scripture portions had been scattered over the district and beyond it. Today, if you were to look in the hole-in-the-wall shelf of hundreds of village homes you would find a Gospel of Mark or of Luke. We know this because we have found that what a villager has paid for he will never destroy. The booklet will probably be brought out whenever anyone is present who can read. Yet in spite of the interest we saw few additions to the visible church.

There were, of course, signs in many lives, particularly among our nearer neighbours, of a sincere love for the Lord. They listened to His Word with reverence, sometimes with a wistful look on their faces as if they longed to break their chains and become one of His own people. They would steal into church, slipping their shoes off at the door, and sitting at the back would follow everything with interest and acceptance. Some of them even brought small sheaves of wheat or rice at harvest time, the first fruits of their crops, offering them shyly and with embarrassment because there was no visible God to lay them before.

We cannot know what God's judgement will be on these feeble acts of faith, this love of His Name, the warm welcome for His messengers in heathen homes, the acceptance of the truth though it might not lead to open confession. He has promised a reward to those who receive a disciple: "He that receives you, receives Me" — and only He knows how sincere the receiving has been. Secret believers; I used to console myself as I watched them with the thought that one day, maybe at His coming again, these fearful believers and many more like them will cry: 'This is our God; we have waited for Him.'

CHAPTER FIFTEEN

Muzaffarpur

Dawn had broken but the sun was not yet risen as I stepped on to the veranda. Looking out over the garden I knew what the hymn writer must have seen when she wrote:

"Still, still with Thee when purple morning breaketh,
When the bird waketh and the shadows flee."

The gravel in front of the bungalow was a delicate lilac and under their canopy of leaves the trunks of the trees were definitely purple. Nor was there a doubt that the birds had wakened, though I couldn't hear them. One and then another darted out from the tamarind tree and beneath the frangipani; rooting among the wax like flowers, a company of Jungle Babblers (Seven Sisters to the Indians) were chattering and grumbling together.

As I walked down the drive I could see the road through the thin patches in the hedge for in the hot season there is little undergrowth to fill the gaps. A group of teaching Sisters from the convent were moving in my direction, their heads meekly bowed, their brown faces dark against their white habits. I knew they were not allowed to talk before church so I hurried across the road and on to the Maidan without looking their way.

At home, we would call the *Maidan* a common. Seen from the air this common would appear round in shape. Our road encircled it, and large bungalows, standing in their own grounds, lined the outside edge of it. In the days of the British rule this had been a racecourse. Here the top strata of British officialdom had lived. For instance, I had just left the compound of the old English church where generations of Britishers – military personnel, civil servants and planters – had worshipped. Alongside it was the Parsonage where Herbert and I now lived. Next door was the Civil Surgeon's residence, a large house standing in its own grounds and beyond it the home of the Holy Cross Sisters. Set in beautiful gardens, their school – the School of the Morning Star – rose above all the rest, its huge star a landmark in this area of low buildings.

Diagonally opposite in the other direction was the Commissioner's huge house and beyond it the bungalows of the Senior District Officer and the Chief Engineer. Then came Circuit House where important Government officials were entertained. And away on the far side, out of our range of vision, were the barracks.

Even at this early hour people were abroad. Two small girls were furtively and hurriedly cutting grass for their cattle, not cutting but digging it out with a trowel, leaving ugly bare patches. They were on forbidden ground; goats might not be pastured on the *Maidan* and grass-cutting was forbidden but I was not in the mood to remonstrate. An Indian gentleman, a high up official out for his morning constitutional, saluted me with his cane. He said nothing to the children so why should I?

People were not stirring in the military quarters over on my left. Those khaki coloured houses were not more than a year old yet were already shabby, the last rainy season having done its worst to the plaster. There were four double lines of them almost opposite our house. How our British predecessors would have fumed over them! Or more probably forbidden their erection, spoiling as they did the beauty of the *Maidan*, but we didn't mind them for they housed the non-Hindi speaking soldiers of the regiment with their families. Quite a few of them were Christians and had brought new life into the church.

I waved to a young woman who had emerged from the back door of one of the flats, bucket in hand, and walked on, exulting in the beauty of the morning. Within an hour or so the sun would be too hot to bear but now the air was fresh, the sky still a cool grey and oh! the trees! In every garden around the *Maidan* as far as the eye could see were flowering trees, not the small trees of our English gardens which bloom in the spring, but huge and magnificent, the Gulmohar with its clusters of orange-red blossoms, the laburnums dropping cascades of lemon yellow, and the pink and white flowers of a species of Cassia. The marvel was that the trees could produce such beauty when everything at ground level was brown and dry. They had access to water that the surface plants could not know; their roots deep down to the water level.

I acknowledged the parable. Impulsively, but from my heart, I cried: 'Lord, make me like a tree!'

I hope that this doesn't raise a smile. I was on scriptural ground after all. 'He shall be like a tree,' says Psalm 1:3 'planted by the rivers of water.' And what about Psalm 92:12-14? 'The godly shall flourish like palm trees and grow tall as the cedars of Lebanon. For they are transplanted into the Lord's own garden and are under His personal care. Even in old age they will still produce fruit and be vital and green.'

I was walking back toward the house now and before my eyes rose the two lines of palm trees planted by some person in the past to line the path to the church.

'You can never be like a tree outwardly,' said a dampening voice within me. 'Not a palm tree, at any rate – tall and slender and straight.'

True. Dumpy and thick I had always been. Compact, people said when they wished to be kind. But I could be like a tree in God's sight. Delighting in His word, sending my roots deep into the sustenance of it, I could find that the spring of living water which is the Holy Spirit Himself, welling up within me, would keep me fresh and green up to old age.

But I was already there – or almost there. Come November, I would see the end of forty years in India. All the colleagues with whom I had worked in my early years had left the field – Edith, Gladys, Kay. Gina had been married and away home years ago and Brownie had lost her life in an air crash outside Delhi. Of my old colleagues only Geoffrey and Monica Lehmann were still in India. They had worked with us in Kachhwa for a time during the 1930s before opening a new hospital in the Himalayan foothills. Indeed, they have outstayed me for, at this time of writing, 1981, they are still there serving the Lord with unabated zeal and devotion.

'Do you realize,' I said to my husband later, 'that come November, I shall have been in India for forty years?'

'What made you think of that now?' he asked.

We were lingering over the breakfast table which had been set up in my angan –a small enclosed place that Herbert had made for me by erecting a bamboo fence and lining it with a quick growing hedge on the quieter side of the house.

'Just thinking back and remembering,' I said. And I quoted: 'Thou shalt remember all the way the Lord thy God led thee these forty years in the wilderness...'

'Are you likening your forty years in India to the wanderings of the Children of Israel?'

'No. Not quite. Their forty years were a sort of punishment, weren't they? Something they had brought on themselves by refusing to go forward with God. They had hurt God terribly and I wouldn't like to do that. But the young ones among them who were going to inherit the land and fight God's battles were not exactly wandering, were they? They were being tested and tried and disciplined, facing hardships in an uncomfortable situation, with monotonous food and sometimes hunger and thirst. But they were being led. They were cared for so that their clothes never wore out and for all their walking, their feet didn't swell. Our experience has been something like that, hasn't it?'

We were silent for a while, watching a red-vented bulbul perched on the edge of the sunken bird bath. His back was toward us and every time he bent to drink he displayed the crimson patch under his tail. A golden oriole darted from the Gulmohar tree and flew across the lawn then a flock of parakeets swooped above us with a flash of emerald and our bulbul flew away.

'I haven't seen the new bird for a day or two,' said Herbert. 'I wonder what happened to him?'

This strange bird had appeared a week earlier. We had caught our breath in wonder when we first sighted him flying across the lawn, his tail streaming behind him like long silver ribbons. He was a Paradise Flycatcher.

'The cook says the other birds drove him away. He had watched them chasing him. He was different, I suppose. It's dangerous to be different. Even the birds find it a costly thing.'

The cook came to remove the breakfast things and Herbert rose and went into the house but I stayed where I was. I was still thinking back and thanking the Heavenly Father who had led us to this place where I had time to think and to dream and to put down on paper the results of my thinking and dreaming.

A sudden quietness had fallen on the garden. The cacophony of sound from the road which daily shattered the peace of early morning for about half an hour had ceased, the yelling of excited rickshaw pullers as they raced and tried to pass each other; the continuous blare of motor horns as chauffeurs, keeping their fingers on the button, insisted on passing them. These vehicles were carrying the children of the rich to the convent school where lessons began at 6.30am during the hot season.

I picked up my notebook which had been lying on the grass beside me. I would do some writing out here so long as there was a spot of shade, which wouldn't be for long. The sun was already high and casting no long shadows of hedge or fence. The scribble in the notebook, defaced by many crossings-out and by arrows pointing to other pages was an attempt to form a book from a series of short stories which had already appeared in the *Light of Life* magazine, written around the lives of one particular Christian family. Though I didn't know it, this was to be my final contribution to literature published in India.

Anyone who has had patience to follow me thus far will have realized that we were no longer in Tirbirwa, no longer tied to the fascinating, exhausting, demanding life of the crowded dispensary. For the past eight years we had been living and working in Muzaffarpur, a large town to the south of our area, a completely new sphere of service. Herbert had been brought here to take over as superintendent of a Leprosy Mission Home and Asylum which our mission had been staffing for some years. The policy of the Leprosy Mission had always been to appoint whenever possible a non-medical superintendent so that doctors and nurses might not be saddled with bookwork and business matters. Although for the past 17 years Herbert's chief task had been the healing of the sick he was not professionally a medical and seemed to be the obvious man for the post.

It had been the opinion of many, including ourselves, that the time had come for us to leave Tirbirwa. The work was taking up more of Herbert's time than he could spare. He was by then the most senior man on the field and since Ernest Oliver's transfer to Nepal he had been secretary of the three-man committee which had assumed the responsibility of Field Directorship. Lillia was now capable of running a dispensary for women, supervised by our doctor, Margaret Owen, who was already visiting regularly the leprosy clinic that Lillia carried on without our aid. The year we would spend at home before proceeding to Muzaffarpur would prove what she could do.

So we had our year's furlough, a happy year in Belfast when our daughter June was married to Jim Hunniford. Michael was now in training as a cameraman with the BBC so we left the three of them in the flat we had rented and set out for our new assignment in Muzaffarpur.

It was not an easy time in which to take up this task. The Leprosy Mission was undergoing a change in policy, phasing out the old method of giving asylum to burnt-out cases who could quite safely re-enter their village homes, and concentrating on prevention of the disease. They were making efforts to contact people in the early stages when the disease could more quickly and effectively be cured. Our Mission doctor, Margaret Owen, with an Australian nurse, was already busy organising village clinics and an ever-growing outpatient clinic in the Home. Now a hospital was to be built on a plot of land adjoining the Home and the supervising of the building was to be Margaret's responsibility.

The Chairman of RBMU, London, Rev. C. Strong, laid the first brick in the foundations and the building began. As the walls got higher, so Herbert's burdens grew heavier. The contractor, who had already been on the job for a year, building the doctor's house, was proving himself to be thoroughly dishonest. Getting anything done in India was normally not without its headaches as one battled with lazy and indifferent workmen, but this man was utterly corrupt and unscrupulous. Herbert became increasingly conscious of something wrong in the building but he didn't know what was wrong. There seemed to be no one to whom he could turn for advice for we knew so few people in the town at the time. He felt helpless in his inexperience.

In the past we had our share of the impossible tasks every missionary must be prepared to face, tasks for which Herbert had not been trained and for which he had no inclination. There was the dispensary, for instance, where we learned to heal the sick by the grace of God and sheer experience. The intricacies of book-keeping also had to be mastered. This task was to assume nightmare proportions as the Leprosy Hospital became established. The Government auditors demanded a receipt for every anna spent and as often as not these were simply dirty bits of paper which could easily be wafted from the desk by the air from the fan and swept up with the rubbish. But nothing had equalled the burden laid upon Herbert by the wily contractor.

One Sunday we were particularly troubled. We prayed together and laid the burden on the Lord. That evening, at the Bible class, a Malayali* Christian called Philip who was a Government building supervisor, said: 'I'd like to come over to the hospital with you tomorrow and take a look at the building.'

His experienced eye soon discovered that while we had contracted for first-class bricks, third-class had been used; the mortar was already crumbling and the building had been fortified with bamboo poles in place of steel rods! A great deal had to be pulled down but Herbert was able

* Malayali people from Kerala who speak Malayalum not Hindi (see p.104)

102

to break the contract after some unpleasantness. He employed a Christian neighbour, a Roman Catholic, who while by no means averse to making a little for himself on the side, was at least doing a thoroughly good job.

Despite this burden of responsibility and apprehension which I shared and which was not to be lifted until four years later, and despite the normal troubles and vexations which dog the steps of every expatriate, I found life in Muzaffarpur pleasant. Housekeeping, for instance, was no longer a problem. The bazaar, a quarter of a mile away, supplied us with meat and fish and with fresh vegetables practically all the year round. In Tirbirwa we had been confined all through the summer months to the gourd-like vegetables – pumpkin, vegetable marrow and cucumbers which meant more thought and ingenuity in the planning of meals. Here the electricity supply though erratic was constant enough to allow the luxury of a two-ring stove with a tiny oven to sit on top. And we had a fridge which meant goodbye to tepid drinking water and white, lard-like butter made from the top of the buffalo milk. We could now store real dairy butter from the city.

Above all, we had our faithful cook who had been with us for seventeen years. I can't think what I would have done had he refused to leave his village home to accompany us. I had always realized with gratitude how blessed I was to have such a helper. Like most of his caste, he was what we would call a born servant. I couldn't recall one instance of his answering me back when I, irritable or impatient, had scolded him unjustly. Yet he was not servile. He had a dignity of his own which was impressive, and at times he could speak his mind. As happened when we took him with us to Calcutta. We were having a great time introducing him to the wonders of electricity (which had not yet reached Tirbirwa), waiting with amusement for his awed ejaculation – Bap array! Oh Father! – as we demonstrated first the light, then the electric fan, then the cooking stove. But when I showed him the electric iron, the mild expletive was cut short. Taking a deep breathe he looked around the kitchen and said to me: 'No wonder your mother can do in a few hours what it takes me a day to do.' Never again could I try to speed him up by telling him what my mother could accomplish in a few hours!

Gahar had always been a nice lad, gentle and without guile, and the years had added to his dignity. He was no longer a raw villager to be taught his trade, ordered about and scolded; he was a responsible member of our household, a faithful and loyal friend. I could trust him to be reasonably clean in the kitchen. I say reasonably clean for probably no Indian cook ever lived whose kitchen would have satisfied the dirt-conscious Western housewife. I rarely entered our kitchen which, as in all old bungalows, was twelve yards away from the house for I agree with the Chief of the Army Medical Corps in India, who was appalled by the number of young doctors who were quitting because of fear of germs, said: 'Trust God, and don't go into the kitchen!'

Stories about servants were rife among the troops, such as the one about the bearer who, caught straining the soup through his master's sock, said hastily: 'Don't be angry, Sahib. It wasn't a clean one!' This may or may not have been true but I remember that in my early days our cook wore his turban as I have already described with a cockade in front and a tail behind. We knew he used this tail for various purposes including wiping the sweat from his brow, so when he was caught straining our soup through this dubious muslin, we ignored his wounded pride and banned the tail.

But Gahar was not of this type. He knew nothing of what the Bible calls eye-service. He was too loyal to do anything behind our backs which he knew we would consider dangerous to our health. We knew that every drop of drinking water had been boiled, however pressed for time he might be, and not once in all the years did I catch him testing the food and putting the spoon back into the pan. Though he never brought himself to the point of baptism, he was a believer in Jesus. The crippling and demoralising superstitions of village Hinduism had fallen from him completely. As we worked together in the house I was able to talk to him of the deeper things of God as to a mature Christian.

The measure of freedom from the cares of the kitchen didn't mean that I had hours and hours of leisure with nothing to distract my mind from my writing. I was still involved with people, not the faceless mass of villagers as in Tirbirwa but with individuals. We were no longer isolated from our colleagues, for instance. We were working in close contact with the team at the Leprosy Hospital, and ten minutes' walk through the residential area behind our house brought us to the home of Aza whose work was the translating into Hindi and publishing of Scripture Union Bible-reading notes – Daily Bread. Later we were joined by Geoffrey and Deirdre Larcombe. They lived in a flat in one of the new estates, near enough to the town for Geoff's work among the students yet within cycling reach of the hospital where Deirdre helped for a time with the nursing.

Until the Kanhouli Church among the leprosy patients and staff became a reality, all the team joined us for worship in Christ Church on Sunday mornings. We would gather in our home afterwards for a cup of coffee with some of the church members and then motor across the town for a service in the Leprosy Hospital. Here we joined patients and staff in singing the Hindi bhajans, singing heartily but not very tunefully for they would take a new hymn, only partially learned, and sing it over and over as they sat around the fire at night until by the following Sunday it was barely recognisable by those of us who had introduced it!

Then we were within reach of our colleagues working to the north of us, even as far as Nepal. Whenever they left their station to go south over the Ganges to Patna, or east to Darjeeling or west to Lucknow, Bombay or Delhi they had to change trains at Muzaffarpur. The waiting times were often long and our house was not a quarter of a mile from the rear entrance to the station so it became a place of rest and refreshment to many.

We had the joy of being the last to wave farewell to friends going home on furlough and the first to welcome them back, and naturally the first to welcome newcomers to the field. Drs Matt and Joanna Peacock arrived one Easter Sunday morning as our service was ending. They had a cup of tea and biscuits with some of our English speaking congregation and then insisted on joining us for the Leprosy Hospital service. Two of the patients were baptised that day. Our new friends were thrilled to have been present at such an exciting occasion and it was not until we were sitting down to as good a Sunday dinner as Muzaffarpur could afford that they confessed that they had had nothing but tea and biscuits for two days, someone having told them not to eat food served from the train!

As train services became more erratic our friends in Raxaul feared to risk boarding the local train scheduled to connect with a main line train in Muzaffarpur at 11pm. They began to leave during the afternoon, arriving with us in time for supper at seven and a pleasant evening together. National friends, mainly hospital staff, arriving unannounced, would shyly produce their own supper. I would serve them with tea and biscuits after they had eaten their curry and chapattis. Many were the happy hours of fellowship we spent with our Indian brethren.

Returning again from their travels friends would invariably arrive at 4.30am. We loved to rescue them, bringing them home for a quick breakfast of toast and eggs and fruit before returning them to the station to catch the 6am local train for the north. We suffered little inconvenience by this service. There was no waiting about for trains which could be an hour late. We could lie in bed until we heard the first faint sounds of the wheels when there was ample time for Herbert to throw on a few clothes, get out the car and be on the platform to greet the travellers and for me to get the breakfast under way.

We owed this convenience to the once important British who, when the railways were being built, refused to have the lines laid through their residential areas. The trains therefore had to make a wide detour before entering the town and we could hear their chug chugging around the Maidan as they made a complete circle.

Not all of our guests were met at the station. Many arrived unannounced, tourists who, taking a stroll through the bazaar between trains, had found our Bible bookshop and been sent by John Matthews to see the English Church. Sometimes Herbert, returning from Patna by the late ferry, would encounter young Europeans and bring them home for the night. Once he brought a couple of French students who had dodged their main party and were sightseeing on their own. We found them delightful youngsters and sat up far into the night talking around the supper table. They took my unspoken rebuke in a good spirit when, finding they were not married, I refused to put them in the same room!

Fortunately for us, although we were on the direct route by train or road to Kathmandu, the Shangri La of drug addicts, we didn't get many of the hippy-type tourists on our doorstep, demanding a night's lodging. (And they did demand, taking these helps by the way as their right). If any of them were taken ill on the station platform the Anglo-Indian officials, mostly Roman Catholics, would direct them to the convent where they received loving but exceedingly bracing treatment from the down-to-earth Sister Superior.

On one occasion we entertained a group from Friends' School, Lisburn – Herbert's old school – seven boys and two masters on their way to Nepal. They had travelled overland with two Land Rovers which the school had donated for the work in Kathmandu. Feeding them stretched my ingenuity to the full for we had not known just when they would arrive. There was no freezer to dive into, no shop just around the corner! But we managed a good meal though the boys were not enamoured of the stewed lychees with custard! We had a delightful evening listening to the Ulster voices as the boys argued amongst themselves about the 'troubles'. Our cook was delighted to serve them, so relieved was he to see young European tourists looking clean and neat, without beards and with short hair!

Periodically came also teams of Operation Mobilisation lads seeking shelter in our house for a couple of weeks while they attacked the town with Gospels and Christian books. Their organisation allowed them to ask nothing more than a veranda on which to spread their bedding rolls. They ate for the most part in the open-fronted 'hotels' in the bazaar but we usually managed to give them some meals, especially on the Sunday, curry and rice with a mango for dessert. These lads were a great challenge to the local Christians wherever they went, transferring some of their own keenness for evangelism. The enthusiasm tended to wane after a while but was heartening to us while it lasted.

We had our share of distinguished visitors, among them Meg Foote, vice-principal of All Nations Christian College. Joyce brought her down from Raxaul and after breakfast with us went to do shopping in the bazaar and to lunch with the staff at the hospital. Meg and I began to talk – and we talked and talked. I forgot that I had intended to put the finishing touches to the lunch table and make a special sauce for the cauliflower. We almost forgot to eat. We have met only twice since then but a link was formed that will never be broken.

One morning an elderly couple stood on our veranda and asked if they might see the church.

'Certainly!' I said, and pushed two comfortable chairs forward. 'I'll send someone to open it up.'

They sat down and I sent a message to the garden coolie who supplemented his wages by acting as church caretaker. I hoped he would have the wit to blow a little dust away while the visitors drank the coffee I ordered.

'We worshipped here for many years,' the man explained. 'I was Commissioner of Muzaffarpur until Independence.'

The wife nodded and smiled. 'We are on a nostalgic tour of the places we knew.' she said.

My husband joined us at this point and the two men were soon deep in a discussion of the changes that independence had brought to India. They agreed that the changes had not all been for the worse. The wife and I were discussing the church.

'We thought it would have been closed down after the withdrawal of the British padre,' she said.

'So it was, for a time,' I replied. 'But when our predecessor came to supervise the Leprosy Home he was looking about for a house and found that the parsonage was standing empty. He wrote to the bishop and was allowed to rent it quite reasonably. As soon as they were settled, the English residents begged him to open up the church for services again.'

'Anglo-Indians, I suppose? They would never settle with a Hindi service, would they? They cling to English as their mother tongue.'

'Yes they came to him of course. There were only one or two left who were not Roman Catholic. But there were the Malayali* families from Kerala who also were much happier with an English service, and over in the barracks were men from other parts of India who were not familiar with Hindi. So with the permission of the Bishop we have carried on with the services. The church is now part of the United Church of Northern India, of course, but they haven't yet an ordained man to take over from us.'

We were now following the men into the church and I was relieved to see that it was swept and dusted. There was nothing to shame me but the tarnished brass of the plaques on the walls. I had given up trying to keep them polished – there were so many of them, memorials to the dead of the Boer War and the 1st World War, of planters killed in accident and quite a few wives who had died so very, very young.

'Did you notice this one?' asked our visitor as she stood in front of an imposing marble slab. 'Look at the list of the lady's good works and virtues. One imagines her to be a serious, pious middle-aged lady and at the end one finds that the poor darling was only eighteen! How they must have suffered in the heat with their voluminous petticoats and tightly laced stays!'

'The old British and French cemeteries are filled with graves of such young women,' said her husband. 'It doesn't happen now, thank God.'

We were now looking up at a magnificent stained-glass window dedicated to the memory of officers of the Bihar Light Horse who had died in the 1st World War, the territorial company who were so kind to us during the Quit India uprising. I said: 'We shall always remember the BLH with gratitude,' and told them what had happened to us in Motihari.

She said: 'My father was a member once. We have a funny story about him. You know that

106

the BLH had no lower ranks – the lowliest jobs had to be done by the officers in turn. One day my father was on sentry duty when a car bringing a visiting general of the regular army drove up, was challenged, and passed through. The BLH officer escorting the general said: "Did you notice that sentry? He is the son of the Archbishop of Canterbury (then Frederick Temple)." The general looked embarrassed, then glum. "Humph! Sorry. Drink, I suppose?" '

So we had been entertaining the granddaughter of an Archbishop of Canterbury. I was thrilled with the visit, not only because of who she was but because the man had reminded me so vividly of the British officials I had known in my early days. Nowadays when it is considered fashionable and clever to debunk great men of the past, derogatory comments are made about the British in India. But whatever atrocities the men of the East India Company may or may not have committed (no one really knows), the administrators of this century were men of integrity. No doubt they drank too much and were even accused of making drinking a status symbol among the nationals. As I heard one Indian lady say bitterly 'If one doesn't drink, one is a nobody!' But they were courteous men, men with a strong sense of responsibility, upright and incorruptible.

Moreover they sought to keep their own particular departments incorrupt from the top to the bottom. While the Civil Surgeon was an Englishman, no hospital sweeper or orderly found it easy to demand a bribe before giving a bedpan to a helpless patient. The simple villager coming to the law courts with his grievance could feel confident that, because there was a 'Sahib' at the top somewhere, he would be dealt with justly. This is not speculation on our part. We had it from the villagers themselves. It was their fear that something trustworthy and powerful had gone from Government institutions that brought them in such embarrassing numbers to Mission hospitals and dispensaries where Angrez* (British) were still in control.

Through the years that have passed since Independence, the villagers must have modified if not lost altogether this distrust of their own people as many administrators and medicals have shown a true concern for the sick and the helpless. As for the image of the incorruptible, man-of–his-word Englishman, that has certainly disappeared. The smashing process was begun by the hippies who began to pour into the country on their way to Nepal and who seemed to be roaming the world without a penny in their pockets. The sight of a 'Sahib' long-haired, unwashed and with dirty bare feet, begging money or thumbing a lift must have been a shock to the simple villagers. More shocking must have been the sight of Englishmen caught smuggling drugs into the country from Nepal and being dragged to the police station.

Perhaps it was as well for the spread of the Gospel that this image of the incorruptible Sahib should disappear. There were times in the old day when I felt it to be a hindrance, taking the glory that belongs to God. Jesus said: 'Let your light so shine that men may see your good works and glorify your Father which is in heaven.' But in our case, however uprightly we might behave, however impervious to a bribe we might be, however truthful, it was taken for granted that it was because we were British. It would not occur to them that they were seeing the power of God at work in a life. Only when a national showed these virtues would it be put down to the amazing, transforming grace of God.

Among our contacts in Muzaffarpur I must not leave out the one who visited us more frequently than anyone else – the Sister Superior of the Convent. During our first two years we had not exchanged so much as a 'good day'. She passed our house every morning on her way to church

---

* means British, but also refers to Indians who adopted western ways.

but there had been no communication. Then one afternoon as we were enjoying a cup of tea before starting work again she tapped at the door. She had come ostensibly to make arrangements for a leprosy sufferer to enter hospital but over a cup of tea the reason for her visit was declared.

'Isn't it lovely that we can now be friends?' she said. The Second Vatican Council was over and Pope John had made many pronouncements. Among other things he had given permission for Catholics to make friends with Protestants.

This was the beginning of a friendship that was refreshing and enlightening. Sister Eleanora was a refreshing sort of person. Austrian by birth, she had a great sense of humour. She was, I think she said, of peasant stock and was down to earth and intensely practical.

'What happened to the pretty Swiss sister you used to have in the school?' I asked one day. She gave an impatient wave of the hand. 'She had to be transferred. She was of no use in the school. She couldn't teach English or Maths, not even sewing. Nothing! She was – what you say? – too heavenly-minded to be any earthly use. All she say is –"All for Jesus".' I gathered that among young nuns this 'slogan' was used to stiffen themselves in hardship much as we in my old Bible College used to say – GMT – (good missionary training) when faced with unpleasant duties.

The friendship was enlightening because we each saw in the other's beliefs and attitude to life something we had not known before. Sister Eleanora especially was strangely ignorant of that which divided us. One evening we had gone at her invitation to see the new school building which was then rising under the vigorous supervision of an elderly building Sister. It was a sultry evening in the monsoon season, warm and humid. I remarked on the heat as I wiped my face.

'What? You, hot?' she exclaimed, plucking at the neck of my dress. 'What about me?' and she pointed to her voluminous, high necked habit and tight fitting veil. 'But never mind, you'll have to make up for it in purgatory.'

'No, I shan't!' I retorted. 'We don't believe in purgatory.'

She stared at me in amazement. 'No?' she ejaculated, then listened while I explained why we rejected the doctrine of purgatory. 'Well,' she said at last, 'when I get to heaven I shall say to the Lord, "It's not fair! Why should I have to go through purgatory and not her?"'

After our tour of inspection of the magnificent, four-storey building (where did they get the money from?) she took us into the house for coffee and displayed with a chid like pride the Hindi Bible lying open on the table in the teachers' sitting room. After Pope John's edict that the Bible should now be read in the vernacular she had been to Bombay and bought for herself a Bible in German.

After this we had many discussions on Bible truths. She would turn up at any time of the day, her face crimson and gleaming, her habit dark with perspiration. Sinking into a chair, she would say: 'I have escaped!' She would have escaped from some trouble with her large staff (there were over a thousand children in the school) or from the crowd of beggars who were continually at her gates, or from a fight with local trades people or workmen or grumbling parents. We would give her a cool drink and we would pray together. Then if she were inclined to linger we would discuss some scripture which one of us might have been reading. One day we brought to her notice the great verses in Ephesians which explain the doctrine of salvation by grace alone. "For by grace are you saved, through faith ... not of works lest any man should boast."

'Goodness!' she exclaimed. 'If we preached that we would get nothing done!'

Even so she affirmed that for her eternal salvation she was trusting in the finished work of

Christ upon the cross and on that alone. And the works that she performed continuously to the point of exhaustion and which put us to shame were done, we were sure, not in order to pile up merit but for a great love of her Lord.

Apart from those who visited us, there were folk who I felt should be visited by me. In the new houses behind ours lived merchants, shopkeepers and money lenders. They were rich enough to have bought us up, lock, stock and barrel and not missed the money. The wives of many of these men were not very attractive or easy to approach. I had loved the village women who never pretended to be other than what they were — poor, illiterate and needy. These newly rich women, while often just as illiterate and unintelligent, were either proud and arrogant, puffed up by the knowledge of their wealth or they were aloof and hostile, perhaps reluctant to speak lest they betray their village origins.

The truly better-class women living in the old, British type bungalows along our road, were easier to approach. They had no inferiority complex and welcomed me as a neighbour or a possible friend. But this didn't make them more responsive when I tried to share with them my joy in the Lord. There was the wife of one of the top lawyers. She had been educated in a Christian college and could produce an apt verse of scripture to illustrate any point in our conversation. She was most intelligent and witty.

'Our name is Sinha,' she said, the first time I called.

'Oh, there are several families in the town by that name,' I said.

She waved a plump hand and laughed. 'Lots of them,' she said. 'More Sinhas than saints!'

We had many interesting conversations over the teacups but she remained staunchly Hindu.

Then there were the Shuklas whom I came to like very much. They were cultured, courteous people, both products of Christian schools. They talked my language and I remember the shock I felt when I first saw their drawing room with its elegant Western furniture. (I had been entertained on the veranda heretofore.) Painted gods looked down from the walls or sat placidly in their niches or even sprawled in embroidered splendour over the chair back covers.

Visiting in the military quarters over the road also had its difficulties, not because of hostility or reserve but because of the language problem. Many of the wives knew only their own language; only those from South India could converse in English. I remember the struggle I had to teach the elementary truths of our faith to a young Indian girl who had arrived from Goa to find herself married to a Christian. Her soldier husband had been attracted to Christianity through his Roman Catholic friends in Bombay but since coming to Muzaffarpur and attending our church he had come to a real knowledge of Christ as Saviour. Herbert baptised him in the river which runs along the compound once the home of C.T. Studd and now empty, the house derelict. Augustine (the name he had chosen to be known by!) was trying to teach his little wife something of what he believed but she was becoming more and more bewildered and I was making little headway. Then a man who had been frightening some of the women alone in the flats, knocking at the windows during the night, was caught in the flat above Augustine's, beaten up and later died. Or so we heard from Gahar. Augustine must have been involved in some way for he and his wife disappeared from the quarters. We didn't like to embarrass Sergeant Major Daniels by asking direct questions for he, though a pillar of our church and a very dear friend, told us nothing. This is the lot that ex-patriots in India must still expect in some circumstances, despite the easier relationship between them and nationals. In time of trouble, especially shameful trouble, the brethren hold together in silence and we know ourselves to be outsiders.

Far more delightful to visit were the women in the Leprosy Home. On the mornings when Herbert planned to remain only an hour or two on the hospital site, I would accompany him and spend the time in the women's quarters. This was a walled-in enclosure, a large courtyard with shady veranda on two sides on to which small rooms opened. Flower beds had been planted along the walls and the women were being encouraged by our nurse Thelma to grow their own vegetables. Here there always seemed to be an atmosphere of peace and quiet. The women would leave whatever they were doing and join me on the shady brick platform where they normally gathered to knit or to chat. Only those who were preparing vegetables for the whole community went on with their task. No sound disturbed the quiet save the occasional shouts of the warden's children at play in their garden over the wall. The only interruption might be the rattling of the chain at the door, heralding the arrival of the cook to collect the vegetables. A wide, sheepish grin would split his poor marred face as he caught sight of me and if the vegetables were not ready he would amble amiably away.

No doubt, this atmosphere of peace did not obtain at all times. Thirteen or fourteen women living together in a confined space could not always be at peace. But however frequent and bitter their quarrels might be (I wouldn't know how frequent) they left no permanent strain on relationships as far as I could see. One reason for their tranquillity could be that they were grateful for the shelter given them. No one in the world could feel more hopeless, more beaten by circumstances, more forsaken by God and man than leprosy sufferers on the streets. Thrown out of home, rejected by friends and neighbours, receiving nothing of friendship from any person – nothing but the momentary pity of strangers and the hastily thrown coin. The loving care of the hospital staff, the special interest shown during times of deep depression which are part of the disease, must have made an impression. Above all they were imbibing the healing words of Jesus. From the first moment of understanding and believing that God loves them, that Jesus so loved them that he died for them, the hopelessness of many lifted. Over and over again we have seen it happen, this transformation from hopeless sadness to quiet joy.

One morning, one of the women told me something of her story. The others had gone to their duties in garden or cookhouse and we were alone. She was a pitiable sight. No toes were left on her feet, her fingers were less than one inch stumps, her face was marred and blotched, her eyelashes and eyebrows gone and she shaded her weak eyes from the light as she looked at me.

'How old were you when you discovered the first numb patch?' I asked her.

'Twelve. It was on my back.'

'What did your parents do? Weren't they frightened?'

'They were more ashamed than frightened. They told me to tell nobody. My father contacted a family in another town and arranged my marriage.'

'Did the family know that you had leprosy?'

'No. No one knew. I wasn't called by my mother-in-law to live with my husband until I was sixteen. They were cultured people and he was still in college. By then there were other patches and the disease showed in my face. My mother-in-law sent me back home.' She paused for a moment and then said simply: 'My own people wouldn't have me either.'

'Then what happened?'

'There was a long fight between the two families and I was sent from one to the other. Once it was a policeman who took me to my husband's house. But in the end both families drove me out.

110

Nobody would allow me in the house.'

I couldn't speak for a moment. The picture of the young girl, cultured and intelligent, condemned to a life among the filthy, terribly deformed beggars on the streets, sleeping in doorways and on the pavement, was too horrible.

'I went all over the country begging,' she went on. 'I went as far as Delhi. I had plenty to eat – people are kind to beggars. Then I came to the Ashram at Hazipur.'

Ashrams are places of rest for pilgrims. They are built and maintained mostly by wealthy Hindus, possibly in the hope of piling up merit for the next life. Or, as our Gahar said dryly, as some expiation for all the money they have amassed by dubious means. The particular ashram where D. found refuge is only fifty miles from Mazaffarpur and near the site of the annual religious mela where thousands of people come to bathe in the holy Ganges, and to buy and sell, and to worship the gods.

'The master was good to me,' D was saying. 'He allowed me to stay and gave me four annas a week pocket money! When I heard about this hospital, he encouraged me to come and he still sends me a little money. I have been back several times when the Doctor Miss Sahib has given me leave for a few days. I meet my old friends and I sing for them – not the old songs but the Jesus bhajans. I tell them about Jesus. How could I do otherwise when He has done so much for me?' She laid a mutilated hand on my knee. 'Memsahib, when I first heard, here in this place, about the Lord Jesus, that he is alive today and that He loves me, it was like a cup of cold water.'

Not a sound disturbed the stillness as she paused. It was as if everything stood still to listen.

'Once when I was singing to the women in the Ashram courtyard, a man came in. He said he lived in the tola over the wall and had been listening to the songs. He had some bhajan books in his hand – said he had bought them from the Christian bookstall in the mela. He and his family and neighbours had tried to sing them but they didn't know the right tunes. He asked me to go over and teach them. So I did. I go and teach them about Jesus whenever I visit there.'

As I listened I thought how terribly she shamed some of us who take our salvation for granted and have no such bright testimony. She misinterpreted the sad look on my face and thought the concern was for her.

'Don't be sad, Memsahib,' she said. 'I have come to the place where I can thank God for allowing me to have leprosy. Otherwise I would never have come to this place of love, never have known my dear Lord Jesus.'

She is not the only leprosy sufferer to have expressed such gratitude. Does it mean that these people, through their affliction, have reached a stage of spiritual experience achieved by few? D. was able to praise God in her suffering – even to praise Him for it. There was no rebellious 'why' which embitters so many Christians in their grief. She had looked at her affliction in the light of God's love for her and His own suffering. She saw that He had used her grief to bring her into a saving knowledge of Him, into a precious fellowship with Him and knowledge of His ways.

CHAPTER SIXTEEN

The Scaffolding Begins to Come Down

"We see not our signs; neither is there any that knoweth how long."

The words leapt at me, suddenly full of meaning from a psalm that had hitherto meant little. It meant something now because it echoed the cry that nowadays was on all our lips, the centre of our discussions whenever we met for conference. And not on ours only. On every mission station the question was being asked: How long? How much time is left to us to prepare for a complete handover of our organisations to the national church?

The Government had made its first move toward the complete nationalisation of all Christian enterprises by putting a ban on the entry of new missionaries. We had managed to bring in an Australian nurse, but this had been accomplished only after Herbert had persuaded the powers-that-be in Patna that because Jean was willing to do leprosy nursing she was invaluable. The official had to admit that as yet nationals were not eager to offer for this essential service. Jean was the final recruit to come to us, that is, as a long-timer. Short-timers were to come, but this was not yet happening.

It was a distressing situation, for the exodus of established missionaries had already begun. Colleagues we had considered absolutely necessary for some part of the work were being driven home by circumstances over which they had no control – ill-health or the helplessness of aging parents, and there was no one to fill their places. Added to this threat to the future of our work, the report came that the Government was contemplating putting a ban on the entry of foreign funds for church or mission work. Our churches had been independent of foreign aid for years but we had mission based institutions which depended a great deal on help from abroad.

There was the hospital at Raxaul for instance - a growing, thriving, up-to-date, first class hospital but needing an enormous number of staff to carry on. Could the church possibly take it over or would the whole concern have to be handed over to the Government? Then there were the orphan girls. Had we in the past received destitute babies offered to us with no thought of our possible expulsion from the country or for the national church who would be literally holding the baby? True we had stopped taking male children some years before but we had a group of young girls who were entirely dependent upon us.

Ought we to be seeing in these movements of the Government signs pointing to the fact that the time was not far off when we could be obliged to hand over everything to the national Christians whether they were ready for it or not? Had we lost sight of the fact that we expatriates (as we were now to call ourselves) were simply scaffolding, an erection from which the Lord could build His church, and not the permanent building? Therefore not indispensable? Would God have to allow our removal one by one until we were forced to act? Would He have to allow us to go through perplexity, bewilderment and heartache because of events which could have been avoided had we seen our signs?

It is a way God must take at times with those of us who really do want to do His will. We are deaf to the still, small voice, blind to the signs, so that He has to use adverse circumstances – sickness or disability – to get us where He wants us to be or to prevent us from doing what He doesn't want us to do.

Another problem, and this touched Herbert and me more than all, was the problem of Mission-owned land and property. Because of the dwindling number of missionaries, several compounds were already unoccupied. The small churches attached to them were still functioning and these, along with the land on which they stood, had been handed over to the national Christians. But alongside each church was this vacant, valuable land, a constant source of temptation to covetousness to a land hungry-people. And Herbert, now Field Superintendent, was responsible for these compounds.

This was a problem on which there was divided opinion. The land must be disposed of. It must not be handed over to the churches. By bitter experience we knew that because of the people's intense desire to own land such an act would precipitate trouble and strife and possibly the break-up of a fellowship. It could be sold in such a way that the Christian community would benefit, and perhaps some old servants. The task of carrying out this plan fell to Herbert.

To free him for this task, a national was found to take over his duties at the hospital and he reluctantly began to make out his plan of action. He reckoned that six months would see him through, but before he could begin there was an interruption, a happening which could have been a sign. I was ordered home for major surgery and our doctors advised Herbert to accompany me. I was glad of this for he had not been well for some time. The break would do him good.

'Our names are not on the passenger list. They are refusing to allow us to board the plane.'

We were at Patna Airport having arranged to fly across India to Bombay under the mistaken (as it turned out) notion that it would give me a speedier and more comfortable journey. Geoffrey Larcombe had driven us to Patna, saving us the trial of an always crowded ferry across the Ganges and we had spent a restful night in the home of Brigadier-General Sailo and his wife. The Brigadier was standing beside me now in the departure lounge when Herbert arrived with the disquieting news. 'I'll see to it,' said this friend.

All through life I have found that at every tight corner, in every frightening situation there is always someone at hand to help. Brigadier Sailo was one of such heaven-sent helpers. A tribal Christian, native of the Mizo Hills, he is one of the many Christians who by reason of their sheer ability and sterling character have risen to high positions in the Government. At this time, he was a new friend to us but a greatly loved one. He was in charge of the armed forces in Bihar and whenever he visited the barracks at Muzaffarpur he would visit us, always in the early morning. Without coat and wearing plimsolls he would take his morning exercise sprinting across the Maidan and after a cool shower would join us at breakfast. Now he was to make us thank God that we had ever known him for had he not accompanied us to the airport that morning we could have been in great difficulty. As it was we were allowed as a favour to him to board the plane though we were guaranteed a seat only as far as Delhi.

At Delhi airport I sat on the baggage for an hour or more, becoming more and more nauseated while Herbert argued with an official and was at last allowed to look at the passenger list. As had happened before, our names had been entered by some up-country clerk as Prit Chand. It needed the alteration of only one letter to turn the name Pritchard into a common Indian name.

At last the clerk decided that we were *bone-fide* passengers and after a hurried meal we took our seats in the plane. Then occurred one of those events which we call coincidences but which are better seen as happenings allowed of God for our protection. A long argument was going on at the foot of the gangway between an official and a lady whose ticket was not for this plane but who was obstinately refusing to move. One of the crew standing by suddenly noticed something wrong with one of the wheels.

We were bundled out and back to the waiting room. Two hours later at five o'clock we were recalled and our journey began. These were the final days of the monsoon, a time of sudden storms and heavy downpours. We found ourselves flying over clouds so white and dense and smooth that we appeared to be looking down on a vast iced cake (in contrast to the usual sea of fluffy cotton wool). At seven o'clock when we must have been nearing Bombay, the pilot spoke to us.

'We are having engine trouble. There is no need to panic. We are about to land at Ahmedabad.'

It was undoubtedly a forced landing. We nose-dived alarmingly through that sea of cloud and landed safely on a flooded airfield, the rain falling in sheets and the water flowing over the tops of our shoes.

Ahmedabad airport had few facilities for comfort, certainly no refreshment bar. The rescue plane from Bombay which we had been promised would bring our supper, didn't arrive until after midnight but there was little grumbling. The atmosphere was friendly and good-humoured, so thankful was everyone to be alive and safe. We had not forgotten that, had the wheel trouble not been spotted, we would have crashed on landing.

Two in the morning was no time of day to go looking for the house where we were to stay in Bombay while irksome formalities were being completed so we curled up on a seat in the terminal and, well bitten by mosquitoes, tried to sleep until five. I spent that day in bed while Herbert wrestled against the officials. Our tickets had not arrived from London and although our names were on the passengers list we were not allowed to travel. In desperation Herbert went to the travel agents who had arranged all our journeys in the past. They at once booked us on a BOAC plane leaving that evening, trusting us though we had no money to pay for the tickets.

As we drove along the waterfront that evening on our way to the airport we thought nostalgically of the old days when we had travelled by ship, not harassed by formalities such as plagued us nowadays, or so it seemed in retrospect. In those faraway days we little thought that the time would come when, because of the closing of the Suez Canal, it would be cheaper to travel by air and we would say farewell for ever to the leisurely trips by boat, the pleasures of wandering along the waterfronts of Port Said and Suez, the seeking for bargains in the bazaars of Aden. A final harrowing experience with a corrupt young baggage clerk at Bombay airport put a finish to the happy dreams.

In March of the following year when I was ready to follow Herbert back to India (he returned after Christmas) I broke my ankle. It was a very bad break and would keep me in plaster for twelve weeks. There were those who urged me to make quite sure of the Lord's will in this further hindrance to my return. Should I consider staying where I was until Herbert had completed his land-selling task and was able to retire and join me?

I must admit that in my weak state (the fall had given me quite a shock) I found the prospect tempting. Herbert was living quite comfortably with the Larcombes who had left their flat in the town and moved into the parsonage. But they were due for furlough in the autumn and then he would be alone. He had made tentative arrangements with the Board for our retirement at the end of 1972 when he believed the land disposal would be completed. I felt that my place was with him until that time arrived.

So I set out on the journey I was to take alone, leaving Ulster on the twelfth of July. There was a short tussle with the security people at Aldergrove who wanted to confiscate my walking stick. It constituted a weapon, they said, but they gave it back when I convinced them that I couldn't walk safely without it.

I spent that night at Redcliffe Bible College with the principal Norah Vickers, an old friend of our India/Nepal days (and as far removed as could be from the old type of Bible College principal I had feared in my young days). I had the added joy of reunion with Bertel Vine after many years. These two friends with Elizabeth Franklin saw me off safely at Heathrow, a kindness I don't forget.

I arrived at Muzaffarpur to find the parsonage most successfully divided into two apartments. Here the Larcombes and ourselves lived and worked together until they left for furlough. It was a happy ending to five years of unbroken fellowship, of relationship without strain. The glory for this must go to the Larcombes who as juniors were completely free from the spirit of rebellion against authority of any sort. There must have been times when Herbert and I, unwittingly, spoke from the supposedly elevated position of the long experienced but if they resented it, their resentment was not apparent.

Geoffrey is now Executive Secretary of our mission in London. No one could have been less surprised than ourselves when he was offered this position for we had proved his potential and his worth during five years lived in the trying atmosphere of an Indian town and the narrow life of a missionary set-up. When they left us for furlough we were facing what was to prove our final and perhaps the most troubled year of our lifetime in India.

It all began with the sale of a few bricks. Indeed, looking back, it seems to me that most of the grievous problems we faced, the bitterest heartaches we endured throughout the years had always begun with bricks and mortar. Or perhaps I should say with land and property. Morgan Derham points out that the first threat to the fellowship of the early church came not through lust or some other gross sin but through property. 'Satan who is ever on the look-out for a possible foothold from which to destroy some ongoing work of God, found it in the hearts of Ananias and Sapphira. As their bodies were being carried out, how many of that first enthusiastic assembly of Christians were warned, finding in their own hearts the beginning of covetousness.'

I have often felt compassion and still do for national Christians caught up and sometimes brought to spiritual ruin by this temptation. For one thing, I'm sure that it springs from the basic, age-old poverty of India, from the desperate desire, inherent in them, to own a little bit of land and so find security. Also it is mission land they are coveting, land, as far as our land was concerned, bought almost for a song from retiring indigo planters at the turn of the century. Some Christians tend to regard this land as their own, bought with money sent for them by Christians abroad. Mission Boards at home naturally consider their representatives, the missionaries, responsible for it. And so these properties becoming increasingly more valuable with the years, have been like millstones on the necks of those in charge of them. There have been times when one has wished that the whole lot could be handed over to the church. But apart from the fact that one has had no authority to do so, there was the knowledge that such an act would increase the headache, precipitate more strife and division. We know also that where property has been handed on to the church, mainly in the larger denominations, now the United Church of N. India, it hangs very heavily indeed on national shoulders. The bishop of our area, a charming Santali Christian and a deeply spiritual man told us that he could not get on with his pastoral work as he longed to do, his time was so taken up with settling quarrels over property, in court and out. He was, in fact, involved in our final distress.

Near to one of our mission stations was the compound of the old English church. There was no church. In the earthquake of 1933 the earth had opened up and swallowed the building, closing over it again. Our colleagues were keeping an eye on the land at the request of the then bishop of the diocese who was quite willing for them to make use of it. They had put up a small building, first as a necessary shelter for the watchman and also with a notion of using it to gather the children of the bazaar for Sunday School. Over the years, as the number of missionaries dwindled, the small, building fell into disrepair and finally became derelict.

One day, the market gardener who was renting the ground came to Herbert asking if he could buy the bricks. Herbert made a bargain with him, took the money and gave him a receipt. As soon as the man began to remove the bricks, a local Christian intervened and ordered him to stop. The man refused and a lively scene ensued which was interrupted by the police. The gardener showed them his receipt, convincing them that he was within his rights. They dismissed the accuser with a warning not to be a nuisance, but he had no intention of desisting. On the contrary, he took the matter to court, accusing the gardener of pulling down a Christian church. For some time a law had been in force for the protection of religious buildings – temples, churches and mosques. Nobody might interfere with any edifice without permission and to pull down a church was a very grave matter indeed.

Three times the Christian brother, whom we will call X, came to us and threatened Herbert also with court procedure if he did not sign a paper affirming that the building the gardener had pulled down was a church. Herbert refused to sign any such paper; neither did he allow these threats to unsettle us. Not at first. We had been assured of God's help by the verses we had been reading on the first critical morning: "The battle is not yours but God's … Ye shall not need to fight …"

This was April 1972.

Then one blazing June day, just after noon, X came again. That summer was one of the hottest we had experienced, or so it seemed. We ought to have been in the hills enjoying a brief respite from the heat, but when the time had come for us to travel I couldn't face the prospect of a thirty-six hour journey in a crowded train, so we had stayed at home. We were in the office when X came, walking in unannounced to resume his threats. The room was in semi-darkness, doors and windows shuttered against the blinding sunlight and the intense heat outside. The hot wind roared round the house and between the gusts the mournful hoo-hoo of a crow pheasant came with monotonous regularity.

The conversation was not lively. Sitting a little apart from the two men I watched an army of tiny ants moving up the leg of a small table, their object the sugar bowl on the tea tray. The scouts who had gone before, to reconnoitre I presume, were moving in the opposite direction, touching noses with each ascending comrade as they passed each other. Soon I would have to get up and frustrate them, slaying the vanguard with a wet cloth. But for the moment I was stunned.

'You have until the 27th to rebuild that church,' X had just said quietly and with no change in his charming smile. 'You have been warned.'

116

On the 20th of that month we heard that he had indeed filed a charge against Herbert. The court of enquiry had been set up, due to begin on the 27th, the task of the enquiring magistrate to sift the evidence and decide whether there was a *prima facie* case or not. Should this be the decision, Herbert would be arrested and would have to remain in jail throughout the court proceedings, for this was a charge that allowed no bail.

The prospect was daunting. Herbert had visited young European drug smugglers in jail and seen the conditions under which they were living, worst of all, seen them on view in the cage-like contraption on wheels in which they had been conveyed from the jail to the court. We had performed small kindnesses for them, buying them fruit and other things from the bazaar to supplement their diet, had helped them get legal defence, written letters to parents and in some cases, hampered by language difficulties, has attempted to show them something of the love of Christ. He little thought the day would come when he might find himself in the same situation.

We knew that others had had to bear such trials. At that moment, all over the world, Christians were languishing in prison for the sake of the Gospel. But the fact that others had borne and come through such an ordeal didn't help much. Ours was not persecution by unbelievers for the sake of the Name of Jesus, an experience which, while being desperate, must have its own glory. There was no glory in being persecuted by a Christian brother driven by covetousness and greed.

We were not really fearful of the outcome in those early days. The charge was so obviously false; it would soon be dismissed; or so we thought, not taking into account the deviousness of an Indian court, the power of bribery and the perfidy of false witnesses, which was foolish of us. We ought to have taken these things into account for we had passed that way before.

As the days passed we became less confident of an early end to the enquiry. Disturbing news kept seeping through. X claimed to have letters in his possession proving that the building was a church. He had borrowed documents from the local estate office which had caused some of our friends who had seen them to look grave. A few of X's friends, obviously recognising that he was becoming mentally unbalanced, became afraid of the length to which he might go and kept besieging us, pleading with us to make a compromise. In vain we insisted that no compromise could be made; the land was not ours to give. X's brother implored Herbert with tears to settle the affair in this way and when refused made this ominous prophecy:

'You must realize that if the case passes the enquiry stage, you will be kept here in prison for at least three years.'

We did not doubt this. We were being reminded of it every day by friendly shopkeepers, minor officials and other acquaintances in the bazaar, and these people knew what they were talking about.

Herbert said: 'God called me to India. If he wants me to stay three more years than planned, I'm ready to do so.'

Looking back, it is interesting to note that among all those sympathisers, most of whom would have considered it a natural course to bribe their way out of such a difficulty, not one suggested to Herbert that we might finish our affair by giving the enquiring magistrate a larger bribe than what he was getting in small instalments from X.

We had friends who did more than sympathise, who tried to help. A Christian police officer succeeded in frightening off completely one false witness (a toddy seller!) and left the others a little nervous. The bishop came from the other side of the province to help us, later sending over

117

documents to prove their ownership of the land and showing that the small building had never been consecrated.

Then the round robins began to come in, long lists of signatures from churches in other parts of our district, from our own mission-founded congregations (including X's own church), from the local Methodists and from an Anglican community eighty miles away. Our accuser had overstepped himself by adding to the original charge that Herbert, being Irish, hated Indian Christians! These friends knew nothing about the building and could not give evidence on that charge but they knew that Herbert did not hate them, that he had always been a friend and brother to them.

Just before these began to come in, I had been reading Psalm 68 in the Living Bible translation.

"O God! Insolent men are risen against me... Show me a sign of Thy favour that those who hate me may be ashamed." These signatures were a heartening sign to us, and as for X, nothing could have daunted him more (or surprised him) than this rising of the Christians in our defence.

But while these efforts helped and warmed our hearts, as did the love of our own church people, they appeared to make not the slightest difference. The case dragged on through July and into August. Over and over again the date was given for the final hearing. We would wait in some trepidation throughout the day for the messenger to bring news of the result only to hear that it had been postponed for a week, a fortnight, a month.

We were beginning to feel the strain. At least, I was. My quiet confidence that God would see us through was now in danger. Not that I doubted His power to save us but, as once before, I was apprehensive lest He should purpose not to do so. Once again I was not well, reacting badly to the heat.

I had no writing assignment to occupy my mind; a short history of the Mission I had been commissioned to write was finished and had been posted. I became restless and depressed.

Then I began to remember how many people had felt that we should not have returned at the time of my operation, how circumstance had added weight to these opinions. A flat we had asked for in readiness for our retirement had been vacated and loving friends had provided furniture and carpets. Then too, Herbert had been released from many of his duties in the mission. The bishop now had a newly ordained national to take over the church at Muzaffarpur. There was nothing but the sale of the land to keep us here.

I now began to plan how I might persuade my husband to leave this to others and retire at once, for only he stood in the way of our going. I don't think the thought had entered his head that we might frustrate the plot against us by leaving the country. He had taken up a task and meant to see it through though it was going to take longer than we had anticipated. He was facing unexpected difficulties over leased land, enduring the frustration of dealing with slow-moving officials. He was hindered all the time by the irritating, couldn't care less attitude of those who don't mind wasting other people's time. After long journeys over execrable roads in the heat to finalise some transaction he would arrive at the appointed place to find that the purchaser had not turned up, nor could he be found. Surveyors who had promised to meet him on a certain day to measure our plots would fail to put in an appearance. There seemed little hope that all would be settled by the end of the year and my heart cried out that then it might be too late.

Then, in late August, X began to visit us again. He came as he had always been used to coming, as a friend, taking a cup of tea and smiling his charming smile. For he had inherited the refined features and the attractive smile of his father who had been a saint and one of our best loved preachers. But it had now become obvious that we were not only against a man crazed with hatred because of frustrated plans and who would stick at nothing to gain his ends but that we were at the mercy of a corrupt judge who was not seeking the truth but was delaying the course of justice in the hope of receiving more bribes.

I think that at this point Herbert also began to be fearful and a little depressed. Perhaps he had unconsciously been pinning his hopes on the officials who were trying to help us. Then one day when I had awakened with a sick fear in my heart, a letter came from Britain from a friend who had been suffering from deep depression for some time. Nothing had seemed to help until she began to read the book *From Prison to Praise*. She had known the theory that praise changes things but had not considered it a principle of life to praise God and even thank Him while still in the dark. She began to say 'Bless the Lord oh my soul' throughout the day even though she had to say it through clenched teeth. And suddenly the depression had lifted. She was well.

As I sat down to answer the letter, a great thankfulness in my heart so that some of my own fear had lifted, I thought of the words: "And when they began to sing and to praise, the Lord set ambushments against the children of Ammon..." Wanting to quote it correctly, I turned up the place in 2 Chronicles chapter 20 and there on the same page, underlined and dated April 1972 were the words which had given us peace at the beginning of our trial but which we were now in danger of losing sight of. "The battle is not yours, but God's."

I shared all this with Herbert and together we reasserted our faith in God to see us through – faith in God alone. Our reading that night in the Psalms gave us fresh comfort. 'For the Lord says, "because he loves Me I will rescue him…"'

The rescue came in early October when Dr Keith Sanders who had been our medical superintendent since Dr Trevor Strong had moved into Nepal, advised us to go home at once. He insisted that I could not face another hot season. He and his wife, Marion, would undertake to settle that which remained of the land transactions.

A month later, the accumulated possessions of the years dealt with, some sold, some given away and the rest packed, the final ends tied and the final accounts handed over, the final goodbyes said to loved colleagues and friends, we left quietly for home, only a few tearful nationals to see us away.

Margaret and Jill took us in the hospital ambulance as far as Barauni, the nearest railway junction of the main line over the river. Having settled us in the train they left us for they had a long return journey ahead of them and it was already late evening. Our faithful cook, Gahar, followed them; his shoulders bowed dejectedly, tears running down his face. We watched him until at last he turned through the gate and was gone.

His was not the last familiar face we saw, however. Into the compartment came Prem, one of our early orphan boys, now working as a dresser in the railway hospital. There was the familiar wide grin on his face as he ushered in his wife (whom we had not met) with the baby girl on her hip. They brought us hot coffee and home-made biscuits and their visit took some of the sadness from our leave-taking.

Sleep didn't come easily that night. Lying on my narrow bunk while the train swayed and bumped across North Bihar and into Uttar Pradesh, I thought back over the years of our service in India and wondered why they had to have such a sad ending. And an almost fruitless ending if we think of fruit as the addition of many new believers to the fellowship. I remembered how our hopes of a harvest had soared during the period of our popularity in Tirbirwa when the crowds had surged around us and many seemed to be ready to take Jesus Christ into their lives. But the seed of the Word had fallen for the most part on stony ground where it had not much earth. We had not come away from there rejoicing, bringing our sheaves with us. There had been no sheaves – only a handful of green blades springing from what had been good ground.

We could have found some consolation in the thought that very few missionaries had left our northern plains of India to the sound of trumpets and with banners waving. Nor were we alone in this experience. I have often contemplated with amazement the faith, the courage and the tenacity of the prophet Jeremiah who preached for a whole lifetime to people who refused to be warned, and felt his heart breaking as he watched his nation slide down to its doom.

Then there was the prophet Ezekiel who was told by God, even as He commissioned him, that people would love to listen to him but would do nothing about it. "Lo, you are to them as one who sings love songs with a beautiful voice and plays well on an instrument, for they hear what you say but they will not do it." Ezekiel 33: 32,33.

And was not the course the Lord's life took an outstanding example of this? First the tremendous enthusiasm for the message, the phenomenal popularity of the Messenger, then the downward trend, love growing cold (from that day many of His disciples went back and walked no more with Him); His enemies' power increasing, criticisms growing, His mission ending in sorrow and the shame of the cross. Yet God turned this seeming failure into glorious victory, used the cross to blight the enemy's power, declaring it the gateway to eternal life for all who would enter.

The risen Christ left but a handful of believers yet on this foundation He has built His Church, living stone upon living stone. Down the years, millions of people, believing on their word, have found new life in Christ and in their turn, many have gone out and many still go out into all the world with the good news of salvation in Jesus.

So I found faith to believe that God has accepted and will make use of the humble service of all those who have served Him in the sterile places of the world similar to ours, who appear to have done nothing but 'heal a few sick folk' and kept the name of the Lord Jesus Christ alive in places where 'other lords' hold sway. With this I fell asleep.

I awoke to find the sunshine streaming into the compartment and Herbert folding his sheet. We were coming into Allahabad station, a familiar sight to me for to this city we had come from Kachhwa annually to do our Christmas shopping.

As Herbert closed the door of the two-berth coupe we had been given for the final stage of our journey to Bombay I sank on to the seat and felt a surge of relief and thankfulness roll over me. From somewhere in my subconscious the words came: "He was better to me than all my fears." I didn't know where I had heard or read them. They sounded at first as if they might be part of Scripture – something from Job perhaps – but I knew they were not. It was some time later that I found the poem containing them.

> "He was better to me than all my doubts,
> Better than all my fears."

For the greater part of that day I sat in my corner watching the familiar northern plains pass without really seeing them – the dun coloured villages, the shady mango groves, the wide river beds. For once, the sight of women going about their daily tasks in villages close to the line failed to rouse in me the conviction that I ought to be down there talking to them about Jesus, a feeling I had never lost since my early days. I was again looking back over the years and realizing to my shame how often I had been a prey to fears – fleeting perhaps but very real – fear of people, of hostile mobs, of disquieting trouble, of pain, of possible destitution because of failures of financial support.

I have no way of knowing if others shared these fears. We don't often air them before others, believing that they reveal a lack of faith or trusting love. But I'm sure that these 'lurking fears' don't leave many of us alone. Otherwise why would the voice of God ring throughout the Bible, challenging all sorts of men, great and small, heroes and cowards to fear not? Fear not! Fear not! And the fact that the 23rd Psalm is a firm favourite with so many speaks for itself, answering as it does the heart's need for reassurance that for the believing heart there is no real cause for fear. In the end, all will be well.

As one nears the end of life's journey, one looks back and sees how seldom the things one greatly feared came to pass. Hostile mobs threatened and drew frighteningly near but never touched us; mission funds fluctuated and dwindled but never dried up; prison gates clanged and rattled but never opened for us. Even during the moments when terror struck, when we felt the waves and billows roll over us, threatening to engulf us, the beloved Lord came to us, striding across the waters. We heard His voice – It is I, be not afraid – we knew His presence and suddenly the storm was over.

As we pass from one experience to another of His love and care, surely we shall find ourselves fortified against the final fear, that fear which, after a lifetime of trust and walking with the Lord, can rear its head as old age approaches – a fear of the valley of the shadow of death. It is not fear of death itself. To the Christian death is but the gateway to Life. It is the fear of that which may lead up to it – the lingering pain, the breakdown of mental faculties, the loss of power to remain independent, the becoming a burden on others.

But as it has been all through life, it is the Word of God that again has power to banish this final fear, to give strength for the 'last great weariness, the final strife'. He hath said: "I will never leave thee nor forsake thee." Therefore we may boldly say: 'I will not fear…'

121

EPILOGUE

I have reopened this testimony after more than ten years, glad of the opportunity to dispel the note of sadness with which I closed it, the expressions of regret because we had reaped no bountiful harvest from the barren fields of North Bihar. I am happy to say that the depression which I at least had felt during the final rail journey across India was short lived. Back to health again, we were soon immersed in the work of the RBMU in Northern Ireland. Herbert had been appointed secretary/treasurer, a post which entailed also the supervising of deputation work. Called upon to speak to church groups and schools all over the province, we had to familiarise ourselves more fully than we had done previously with the activities of our colleagues and national brethren in other fields – in Peru, Nepal, Irian Jaya and Zaire and were soon seeing ourselves as part of the whole outreach of the Mission.

This led us to look at our past service in Bihar from a different standpoint. We were no longer focusing our prayers and interest on the tiny area where we had worked, we saw our past service also as part of the outreach of the gospel to the whole of India, our healing ministry as part of the ministry of the whole church. Now, relying on letters and literature sent to us by the Evangelical Fellowship of India and by Operation Mobilisation, we were watching the growth of that church with excitement. We knew ourselves to be part of it. Because of our past contribution and our daily prayers for it we were sharing in its triumphs and setbacks, and one day we would share in the joy of harvest, when sower and reaper shall rejoice together.

So we followed prayerfully the growth of the India Evangelical Mission, an organisation wholly national which at its inception in 1965 had not one missionary but today has over two-hundred-and forty workers in India and abroad. We watched also the phenomenal growth of the Friends' Missionary Prayer Band, an association of churches and prayer groups scattered over Tamil country in the south which has sent, up to date, four hundred missionaries to hard and sterile areas of North India, each worker and family supported by the sending group.

We watched the same thing happening among the tribal peoples of the north-eastern states (the old Assam) who are not only turning to the Lord in large numbers but are sending their own missionaries to other tribal areas of India. Most of the support for these workers comes from the custom of each housewife setting aside a handful of rice before she cooks each meal.

Some years ago, Theodore Williams (a national, despite the name!) reporting on the growing spirit of evangelism among these people of the southern, eastern and western states of India, said: 'The word of God is blowing over India today bringing new life to God's people, a new independence of foreign support and above all, a new sense of mission.' But he added these poignant words: 'The churches of the Hindi belt remain untouched.'

The Hindi belt is the northern and central region through which flows the sacred River Ganges, the stronghold of a rigid Hinduism. In one corner of that region live the small congregations with whom we of the RBMU have worked and worshipped, churches planted, for the most part, at the turn of the century. They are all included under Theodore's sad indictment.

But now there is a stirring among them. We have been able to thank God for allowing us to experience the joy of seeing others – national workers – reaping where we have sown. Some years ago, two couples, members of the above mentioned FMPB travelled up from the south and settled in Siwan, two thousand miles from their homes and families. (Siwan is the place where the Christian community almost destroyed itself during the final years of the 2nd World War.) After a few years of what we know must have been hard and unrewarding work and witness, the evangelists have had the joy of seeing a church building rising on ground dedicated for this purpose by Walter Corlett in 1938 and which was still unoccupied in 1972 when my husband, having sold the deserted compound, left the plot available. The old congregation had met for worship in the assembly room of the school and never saw the need to build their own church. Now new life has come to the remnant of that congregation and others who have settled there. Small groups of interested people are meeting in nearby villages for worship and teaching. Also, since the 'Go 83' campaign of the Operation Mobilisation group, correspondence courses of Bible Study are going out to five hundred or more Biharis and the response is encouraging.

To the northwest of Raxaul, bordering on the Kingdom of Nepal, live another tribal (aboriginal) people called Tharus. They are an interesting and a fine people as we have cause to know, for Lillia, our dear and extremely capable helper in the dispensary at Tirbirwa has her roots there. During the years after the 1st World War, her mother, widowed and with two small children, trekked south in search of work and was befriended by two of our earliest missionaries, Mr and Mrs Wynde. They gave her work and finally settled her and her family, now professing Christians, in Gopalganj.

Later, missionaries penetrated the forest areas from which they had come, setting up an outstation at a place called Harnatar. Dr Cecil Duncan worked there for a time in the late twenties before founding the hospital at Raxaul, now called the Duncan Hospital. The work closed down later for lack of personnel and as far as I know there had been little result of the evangelism done there.

However members of the FMPB are settled in Harnatan and have seen encouraging results. A small group of believers now gathers regularly for worship and teaching. Julia Patton, calling on them on her way home from the Don, spent a night in the home of one of the believers. Although they had been baptised but a few months, she found them spiritually alive and mature, aware of their responsibilities as Christians to live lives worthy of the Lord and to share their faith with others.

The Don, a wide fertile clearing in the forest north of Harnatan, is cut off from the rest of the country during the monsoon periods. Here is another small congregation gathered from among these once 'hidden people'. A church planted in the sixties through the zeal of the Raxaul Hospital staff and still cared for by them as far as possible but the wind of God, now blowing so powerfully over other tribal areas, drawing hundreds into the fellowship of the Christian church, has not yet swept through the whole Tharu community. Much prayer is needed for these two churches hidden away in the forests of the Tharushat.

It might have gone down ill with the small church in the Don had the Duncan Hospital been forced to close when foreign missionary personnel dwindled rapidly and, because of Government legislation, foreign funds for church or mission activities were greatly curtailed. Thankfully, another national organisation, the Emmanuel Hospital Association came to the rescue, taking over the Duncan and eleven other hospitals, including those at Kachchhwa and Robertaganj with which I had been connected in my early days. Because EHA is a legally registered body, not controlled by mission or church, it is permitted to receive funds from abroad and to recruit expatriate personnel who will bypass the Government ban on foreign missionaries as such. It is led by Mr Lalchuagliana, himself a tribal Christian from Mizoland who gave up a good position in Government at the call of God. This association, deeply Christian and evangelical in basis and aims, merits our prayerful support. It desperately needs the support of Christians in Europe and America, many of whom have not yet realised that interest must not now be centred wholly on missionaries who have gone out from their own churches but on national organisations such as I have described who are struggling in their poverty to spread the Good News of Jesus Christ, to heal the sick and to succour the poor.

So my old dreams, formed among the frustrations of village evangelism in the thirties, are coming true. Gone are the days when converts huddled under the missionary's wing on the mission compound, alien to the townsfolk and villagers alike. Christians are now found in all walks of life from Government administrators (Brigadier Sailo who was so good to us when I was sick, is now head of one of the North Eastern States), doctors, nurses in Government hospitals, teachers in schools and colleges to technicians and manual workers in factories and workshops. That for which I longed and prayed so fervently has come to pass. Even in the vast sterile area of North Bihar, there are now Christian families scattered in outlying villages and I am sure the same conditions obtain in the wide, populous areas around Benares and Allahabad where I first worked and knew such frustration of spirit.

The scaffolding of foreign missions is being stripped away but the national church still stands – and grows. The fields are still white and ready to harvest, not only in India but across the whole world. The Lord still calls for labourers to work in His harvest. One day, all labour on earthly fields will cease and the true harvest will be revealed. Then reaper and sower will rejoice together as He, the Lord, reaps the harvest He has sown.

In the 23rd Psalm, David speaks with confidence of the time when he must enter the Valley of the Shadow of Death, knowing that the Lord would be with him. It is uncertain whether he was referring to any of the tremendous trials of darkness that most of us experience at some time or other or whether he meant the 'last great weariness, the final strife' to which I have already referred. If the latter, then during the past two years (1984-85) Herbert and I have walked together through the Valley of the Shadow of Death knowing that, when we reached the end of it, Herbert would walk on into Light, the Eternal Light of the presence of the Lord he loved. But I would have to turn back.

We knew that this parting was inevitable because of the nature of his final illness, knew that there was no cure for it, therefore no treatment. He might live three years at the most. Not that we accepted the verdict at the time. Our times are in His hands. God Himself would give the verdict. Friends in many parts of the world were praying for his healing. At his own request, several Friends, men and women of faith and prayer gathered in our home one Sunday afternoon to pray with him and for him. They anointed him with oil and waited on the Lord for the healing of His servant.

But although from that quiet Sunday afternoon there was a definite improvement in his general health, a new hope and a new confidence in his prayers, the disease continued to take its course. Once again, the Lord was saying to us: "My grace is sufficient, for My strength is made perfect in weakness."

It was toward the end of 1983 that the first symptoms had appeared. He who had a glorious singing voice lost the power to sing. He grieved a little over this but still enjoyed the singing of others, beating time gently with his hymn book. Then his speech became garbled and swallowing difficult. In March 1984, the neurologist at the Royal Victoria Hospital in Belfast diagnosed his trouble as the dreaded Motor Neurone disease, reckoned to be one of the worst of spinal nerve diseases. There is a deterioration of the nerves of the spinal cord and, as these nerves die, orders from the brain are not received by other parts of the body. Muscles become atrophied and in total Motor Neuron this leads eventually to paralysis of the whole body. We were thankful that Herbert's trouble remained confined to the muscles of throat and tongue. Even so, the fatal nature of the disease had its way. On May 27th 1985, after only eighteen months of growing weakness, the Lord took him Home.

Ending my testimony, I would like to answer some of the questions that have been put to me, questions which may also have risen in the minds of readers who have had the patience to follow me this far. For instance, after all my declared convictions concerning the power of the Word of God to comfort and to heal, did we find that word just as potent as we walked through the dark valley? Did we find the promises of God on which we had leaned all our lives to be trustworthy? Did He prove His grace sufficient to keep Herbert in perfect peace as he faced imminent death? Did I find His grace sufficient, giving me strength in a testing quite different from any I had experienced in India, the strain of coping with all the work of a house while caring for a sick husband? In the face of my dear husband's mental and physical suffering, am I still confident that "all things work together for good to them that love God, to those called according to His purpose"?'

To these questions, my answer is 'Yes, and again Yes'. Herbert faced the verdict that he was suffering from an incurable disease fortified by his unshakable faith in the Word of God, in absolute trust in His love and wisdom. He was given grace and strength and even joy throughout his ordeal, bearing the frustrating handicap with patience, serenity and without a trace of self-pity. Cut off from communication with others, he was drawn into a new and very close relationship with the Lord. He spent hours of each day in his old office, reading the Bible or seated in front of the board on which he had fixed photos or the names of all the people for whom he prayed daily.

When the days grew long and wearisome because his eyesight was failing and he could no longer read, when he could swallow practically nothing and every meal was a nightmare to me, the look of peace never left his eyes, the smile which was the only response he could make when visitors spoke to him, was there to the end. During the final few weeks of his life when his mental faculties began to weaken so that he became a different person with a different attitude, sometimes almost hostile, toward those he loved best, he still found peace in prayer. I who could read his lips am sure of that. On the last day of his life, having developed some pain which we could not locate but which caused him to be restless and anguished, he cried silently: 'Lord, I love You. Help me now.'

And he was helped. He was taken to hospital that morning where they relieved him of his pain but he soon lost consciousness. Just before midnight, as his much loved daughter June watched by his bedside, he died, quietly and peacefully. He had passed through the Valley of the Shadow of Death and the Lord had been with him, as He had promised, all the way. This is why we sang joyfully at his funeral service the hymn he had loved me to sing:

"Thine be the glory, risen, conquering Son,
Endless is the victory, Thou o'er death hath won."

Another question I have had to answer more than once is this: 'Why should God allow this trial to come to you and Herbert after all your years of service for Him?'

The answer to this question will make a fitting final word of my testimony. 'Why not? God never promised to shield us from all suffering but only to keep us in it and to bring us through it. He has a purpose in every experience He allows us to go through.' To one friend, I added: 'Even at my advanced age there must be something I need to learn.'

'Not you,' my friend replied. 'You don't need anymore harrowing experiences to make a good Christian of you.'

But simply to come up to people's notion of what constitutes a good Christian is not enough. God demands more than that and I myself had wanted more. All through my Christian life I have prayed that I might become more like Jesus. I longed for His patience and His gentleness because I knew that these graces were lacking in me. I recalled for my questioner occasions when I had shed tears of mortification after losing patience with and hurting some poor Indian villager, shocking my Christian helpers and bewildering the patients. (Thoughtful people will not need to be told that lack of patience, a short temper and irritability are the sins we repent of most frequently and bitterly because they lead more than others to mortifying situations!)

Yet I have gone on praying, for I have always been aware of the possible result of neglecting these fruits of the Spirit – love, joy, peace, patience, kindness, gentleness by not caring, by remaining unrepentant, by excusing myself and blaming circumstances whenever I have displayed before others just how hard, how unripe these fruits are in my life. I knew that, without the sunshine of God's forgiveness warming them all the time they would never ripen and at the end of my days, when self-control weakens, I could find myself to be a cantankerous old woman and, as the 17th century nun said: 'A sour old woman is one of the crowning works of the Devil.' I believe that God is bound by His own Word to answer every prayer we make from a believing, humble heart and in the name of Jesus. Moreover, when that prayer is a plea for more likeness to His son, He will use every experience His love allows us to suffer in order to answer it. And He will go on doing so for as long as we live. So there is no room for the querulous, faithless 'why?' in our minds and hearts. However painful the process may be that God is using at the moment to answer our heart's desire, let us accept it as from Him who loves us and desires only our highest good. More even than accepting, let us co-operate with God in His purposes, offering our suffering to be used as He will, for our own good, for the good of others and for His dear Name's sake.

Elizabeth Pritchard

126

END NOTE

Reading through the last few chapters of Mum's manuscripts and some of her old diaries I am reminded again of the essence of her character. First the passion with which she lived her spiritual journey and her desire to "be more like Jesus", especially in the areas of patience, kindness and gentleness. Her gifts of preaching and teaching, especially on practical Christianity were appreciated both by Indian colleagues and hearers young and old here in the UK. Many loved her for her humour, wisdom and straight talking. Her generous hospitality was well known far and wide, as were her efforts to maintain relationships with friends spanning her lifetime. Fellow missionaries valued and enjoyed her letters that showed a real understanding of their work and she never forgot her "thank you" notes! In her latter years she often wondered if the Lord was keeping her here until He had perfected her, but perhaps it was for us to enjoy her for as long as possible.

Mum lived with us in Lisburn for nearly five years after Dad's death, continuing as much as possible to worship with the Friends in the Meeting House and to join with her beloved ladies' Bible study group where she shared her wisdom and knowledge and was loved and upheld in return. Old friends were generous in having her to stay, and Lakeside Residential Home, owned and supported by friends in our own Great Victoria Street Baptist Church, offered a home from home when needed. When Jim's work necessitated moving to Randalstown, Mum made the decision to move to Lakeside permanently so that she could remain near her Lisburn friends. Many continued to call with her regularly and the "Bible Class girls" faithfully chauffeured her to the venues. She settled into Lakeside and its spiritual environment with a surge of renewed vigour as she returned to her Bible teaching and preaching days, sharing God's Word with fellow guests on a Saturday morning and being unofficial hostess to the committed ministers and caring groups who took weekly services in the home.

We appreciate the love and care given to her by the staff over those ten years till failing mobility, ill health and a fractured femur kept her in the elderly care unit of the Royal Victoria Hospital for six months until a bed became available in the nursing home of our choice, just a stone's throw from our house in Randalstown. In God's provision Mum was welcomed into Drummaul that July morning by Martha, a senior staff nurse with a boundless capacity for loving. Later the care girls trouped in to make her welcome and as I left that evening she beamed up at me from her pillows and said, "I think I shall be very happy here".

On 25th November 2002 Mum passed away peacefully, aged 96, in Drummaul House, where a short service was held two days later before she was laid to rest in the lovely old Friends' burial ground on Balmoral Avenue in Belfast. Finally her extended family and friends gathered in the tranquil surroundings of the new Meeting House in Lisburn to give thanks for her life and in the unique manner of Friends many were able to share in the uplifting meeting. We would like to thank you all for making it such a special farewell.

Many people played a big part in Mum and Dad's life. They always maintained that the Lord provided special people for each furlough's needs. Similarly, in her later days, Mum's life was enriched by many visits and letters. We would like to thank, for their support and love they brought to Mum's life:-

- The R.B.M.U. family,
- The Quaker family and Moyallon Campers,
- The Bible Class ladies, especially Elizabeth Scott who was a spiritual daughter to her,
- Lakeside and the folk who commit to its spiritual health,
- Drummaul House,
- And all the family, neighbours and friends who over the years made life that bit brighter for us all.

Our sincere thanks also to Helen Kinkead, Martin Mail, Elizabeth Scott and the Friends Home Mission Committee for undertaking the task of transforming Mum's typed notes to what we have today.

Lastly Michael, Sally, Jim and I are eternally grateful to Mum and Dad for the priceless heritage of their faithful and unceasing prayer for us their children, their grandchildren and great-grandchildren. We are all the poorer for their passing.

"To God be the glory"

June Hunniford (neé Pritchard)

The Regions Beyond Missionary Union (RBMU)

The Regions Beyond Missionary Union originated in 1873 from the work of the revivalist preacher Henry Grattan Guinness (1835-1910), a nephew of the founder of the brewing empire. He, with his wife Fanny established an interdenominational missionary training institute. By 1915, 1500 missionaries had been trained and sent around the world, some joining established missions and others forming their own societies. The Guinness family connection with RBMU lasted into the 1970s through the support of Henry Grattan Guinness's grandson, Gordon Meyer Guinness (1902-1980).

In 1888 the Guinnesses launched a new mission to Central Africa, the Congo Balolo Mission. To encourage support the Regions Beyond Helpers Union was formed in 1892 and membership reached 11,000 by 1897. In 1899 the first missionaries were sent to the Bihar region of India, and in that same year the name of the Institute was changed to the Regions Beyond Missionary Union and the RBMU was incorporated in 1903. Financial difficulties in the early twentieth century meant the mission had to restrict its activities to Congo and India. After the Second World War the work was expanded with the absorption of the Peru Inland Mission (1948) and entry into Kalimantan (Borneo, 1948/9), Irian Jaya (1954) and Nepal (1954, with the United Mission to Nepal). Despite, and in some ways because of, the mission's successes some began to question the role and purpose of the mission, especially in relation to the indigenous churches. The wide diversity of fields stretched resources and administration and so the idea of co-operating with other similar agencies became attractive. The North American councils (formed in 1948) took a different view and in 1979 the London based RBMU UK split from its overseas councils, the latter operating as RBMU International. In the UK the mission became more involved in joint projects and in 1980 shared office premises with other agencies. It still sought ways to maintain its own identity and considered expanding to new areas such as Pakistan, Thailand, and the Philippines, but in 1990 the work in each area was passed to new or existing agencies. The last RBMU missionaries stopped work in 1991.

REGIONS BEYOND MISSIONARY UNION ARCHIVE:– is held by the Centre for the Study of Christianity in the Non-Western World, New College, University of Edinburgh.
WEB= http://www.mundus.ac.uk/cats/3/42.htm
Reference code(s): GB 0237 Edinburgh University, CSCNWW 33
Title: Regions Beyond Missionary Union c1872-1991
Extent and medium: 72 boxes, 4800 slides, 30 films
It includes three books by Betty Pritchard (missionary in India)*:
Sown in the Dust (1955?), The Sword of Elijah (1968), and A Sword at the Heart (1970).
These are contained with two other books: Typical Pictures of Indian Natives (1897); and Across India at the Dawn of the 20th Century (Lucy Guinness, 1898).
*Another book which was written about the RBMU is not in the archive:-

'For such a time' by Elizabeth Pritchard, (Eastbourne: Victory Press, 1973).
Adam Matthew Publications have some information about the RBMU archive on their internet site.
WEB=http://www.ampltd.co.uk/digital_guides/regions_beyond_missionary_union_parts_1_to_5

Also for further information:-
RECORDS OF BCMS (Bible Churchman's Missionary Society)
ARE HELD AT BIRMINGHAM UNIVERSITY
WEB= http://www2.special-coll.bham.ac.uk/catalogue_handlist_BibChMSoc.htm
The Bible Churchmen's Missionary Society was founded in 1922 following a division within Church Missionary Society. Its earliest missionaries were sent to Canada, China, Burma and Africa. It changed its name first to BCMS Crosslinks in 1990 and subsequently to Crosslinks. In 1925, the society founded the Bible Missionary Training College in Bristol to train its missionaries and it subsequently opened Dalton House for training women. The men's college was renamed Tyndale Hall in 1952 and in 1972 it merged with Dalton Hall and Clifton Theological College to become Trinity College.
RECORDS OF The Church of England Zenana Missionary Society
ARE ALSO HELD AT BIRMINGHAM UNIVERSITY
WEB= http://www2.special-coll.bham.ac.uk/catalogue_AM_archmiss_misssoc.htm
Zenana was founded in 1880. Its main aim was to evangelise the women of India by means of normal schools [teacher training colleges], zenana visiting, medical missions, Hindu and Muslim female schools and the employment of Bible women. The Society was to work in close co-operation with the Church Missionary Society. In 1957 it amalgamated with CMS.